Praise for *The Best M*

"This book is more than fun homespun sto
cine. You may see yourself in its mirror, yet ...., , ...
better for it in the end."

from the foreword by **Jerry B. Jenkins**, *New York Times* bestselling
novelist and biographer

"Once again, Dr. Larimore has provided a delightful book full of
sound wisdom and fascinating characters. Enjoy a great read!"

Ruth Graham, author of *Forgiving My Father, Forgiving Myself: An
Invitation to the Miracle of Forgiveness*

"With grace and humor, Dr. Walt Larimore delights the reader with an
honest and heartwarming journey of discovery. From his early days as a
young doctor, this memoir takes a poignant look at what it means to be
a Christian physician, friend, husband, and father. *The Best Medicine*
is an enjoyable view of life through Dr. Walt's compassionate eyes."

Jan Drexler, bestselling author of *Hannah's Choice*
(Journey to Pleasant Prairie series)

"Warm, inviting, and nostalgic. Dr. Walt Larimore brings to life a
rich cast of characters and their Central Florida home in his tale of
finding a fresh start and true healing."

Liz Johnson, bestselling author of *The Red Door Inn*

"Dr. Walt Larimore has written a delightful look at the life of a small-
town doctor chock-full of interesting characters and medical tales.
This is the kind of book you want to sip like sweet tea but wind up
drinking in a satisfying gulp. You will enjoy the journey!"

Chris Fabry, Moody Radio host and author of *A Piece of the Moon*

"I was raised a small-town girl—one who moved from the low country of coastal Georgia to the 'big city' in Central Florida. *The Best
Medicine* resonated with every fiber of my being. I have always enjoyed small-town, front-porch tales, and Dr. Walt Larimore's book
fits the bill perfectly. I guarantee that when you read this collection
of stories that reflect on his family's move from Bryson City, NC,
to Kissimmee, FL, you'll laugh, you'll cry, you'll yearn for a simpler
time—and you will desire to know the daily God, the God of our
days, more intimately."

Eva Marie Everson, CBA #1 bestselling author, award-winning
speaker, and president of Word Weavers International, Inc.

"After reading *The Best Medicine*, I could settle for calling Walt Larimore an engaging storyteller. But he's more than that. Dr. Larimore connects with people through their stories and truly cares about their life experiences. In *The Best Medicine*, he shares a delightful assortment of stories in a way that made me feel as if I was sitting across the table from him, not reading a book. I laughed. I cried. And I found myself caring about people I've never met."

Beth K. Vogt, Christy Award–winning author
of the Thatcher Sisters series

"Hope and humor show up in unexpected places, as Dr. Walt Larimore's unique and delightful stories show. With grace and the astute heart of a physician intimately engaged with not only his patients but also his town, Larimore offers an extraordinary glimpse into the heart and soul of how healing happens and how hope can be found in the middle of unlikely circumstances. As a tenured nurse, I can attest to the difficult truth that not all cases end well, and Larimore does not shy away from the hard things. But he balances these stories with the truth that all things work for good when the Lord is in the midst. Highly recommended, not just for health professionals but for anyone seeking assurance of good and grace, even in uncertain and tremulous times."

Amy K. Sorrells, author of *Before I Saw You*

"I laughed, I cried . . . really! Such a good book! This should be required reading for family medicine residents, probably even all medical students. It paints a real (but entertaining) picture of a man who, by growing in his relationship with God, grew in his ability to be a real physician, husband, father, and friend. I can't wait to read the next volume!"

James D. Collier, MD, former assistant surgeon general for
healthcare operations, United States Air Force

Praise for the Bryson City Series

"With homespun warmth, my friend Dr. Walt Larimore tells stories that integrate the science and art of medicine. Walt is a brilliant lifelong learner who is patient centered. *Bryson City Tales* portrays medical practice as something deeply personal, relational, and spiritual."

Randy Alcorn, bestselling author of *Deadline*
and *The Treasure Principle*

"Walt Larimore has the gift. His fine book brings before the reader a vivid world inhabited by colorful people. We see the tragedy and triumph of their lives, and like a master, Doc Larimore employs the old show-business adage, "Make 'em laugh—make 'em cry!" If you are seeking a book that delights and informs, you need look no further than *Bryson City Tales*."

Gilbert Morris, bestselling author of the House of Winslow series and the Appomattox series

"How does a young doctor manage to integrate his background of high academic medical training and simple Christian faith into the hurly-burly of established human relationships in a mountain community? This sounds like heavy stuff, but it turns out to be light—almost hilarious—reading."

Paul Brand, MD, bestselling coauthor (with Philip Yancey) of *Fearfully and Wonderfully Made* and *The Gift of Pain*

"I feel strongly that life is too short for me to read books that fail to move me deeply or take me to places I've never been. *Bryson City Seasons* succeeds wonderfully on both counts."

Joe L. Wheeler, PhD, editor of the bestselling Christmas in My Heart series

"Reminiscent of authors like Philip Gulley, Larimore keeps readers laughing through one chapter and teary-eyed through the next."

Christian Retailing magazine

"Larimore is consummate storyteller. This truly gentle man weaves a story of God's ever-present love and care for the people in this mountain community. So, build a fire in the fireplace, grab a cup of hot chocolate, and settle down for a delightful afternoon in Bryson City, North Carolina. When the afternoon is done, you'll be homesick for more."

Linda Whitlock, ChristianBookPreviews.com

"Fans of House Calls and Hitching Posts and James Herriot's beloved stories will adore the sometimes hilarious, often poignant, and always engaging books in the Bryson City series. Each is filled to the brim with the adventures—and misadventures—of Dr. Walt Larimore in his roles as Christian family physician, wilderness doctor, and county coroner. If you love the day-to-day drama and humor of small-town stories, kick back with the endearing characters of Bryson City and make yourself at home."

DoubleDay Book Club

THE *Best* *Medicine*

THE *Best Medicine*

TALES OF HUMOR AND HOPE FROM
A SMALL-TOWN DOCTOR

Walt Larimore, MD

Revell
a division of Baker Publishing Group
Grand Rapids, Michigan

© 2020 by Walter L. Larimore, MD

Published by Revell
a division of Baker Publishing Group
PO Box 6287, Grand Rapids, MI 49516-6287
www.revellbooks.com

Printed in the United States of America

Library of Congress Cataloging-in-Publication Data
Names: Larimore, Walter L., author.
Title: The best medicine : tales of humor and hope from a small-town doctor / Walter L. Larimore, MD.
Description: Grand Rapids, Michigan : Revell, a division of Baker Publishing Group, 2020.
Identifiers: LCCN 2020014810 | ISBN 9780800738228 (paperback) | ISBN 9780800739904 (hardcover)
Subjects: LCSH: Larimore, Walter L. | Physicians (General practice)—Florida—Kissimmee—Biography. | Medicine, Rural—Florida—Kissimmee—Anecdotes. | Family medicine—Florida—Kissimmee—Anecdotes.
Classification: LCC R154.L267 A3 2020 | DDC 610.9759/25—dc23
LC record available at https://lccn.loc.gov/2020014810

Chapter 1, "Near Death," is adapted from Walt Larimore, MD, *Bryson City Seasons: More Tales of a Doctor's Practice in the Smoky Mountains* (Grand Rapids: Zondervan, 2004), 299–302. Used with permission.

The names and details of some people and situations described in this book have been changed or presented in composite form to ensure the privacy of those with whom the author has worked.

The proprietor is represented by WordServe Literary Group. www.wordserveliterary.com

In keeping with biblical principles of creation stewardship, Baker Publishing Group advocates the responsible use of our natural resources. As a member of the Green Press Initiative, our company uses recycled paper when possible. The text paper of this book is composed in part of post-consumer waste.

20 21 22 23 24 25 26   7 6 5 4 3 2 1

Dedicated to

John R. Hartman, MD
Florida's Family Physician of the Year—1997

Let us tell [the public] candidly that, although [the physician's] resources are in reality great, and that often, by their proper administration, dangers are diminished; yet without the help and blessing of Him who gives knowledge to the physician, and health to the sick, these resources are feeble and powerless!

Thomas Dent Mütter, MD, "The Father of Modern Cosmetic Plastic Surgery," in his charge to the graduates of Jefferson Medical College, Philadelphia, March 8, 1851

Contents

Contents

Foreword

DON'T LET THE HOMEY TITLE and subtitle fool you. While Dr. Walt Larimore's curl-up-by-the-fire memoir may have elements that remind you of British veterinarian James Herriot's *All Creatures Great and Small*, it bears a significance all its own.

Dr. Walt is a physician, not a vet. And while he may have earned his chops in small-town medicine, he went on to become one of the most celebrated family doctors in the United States.

But the difference goes much deeper. Oh, *The Best Medicine* has all the warmth and humor of *All Creatures*. Funny and heartwarming stories abound but be careful. You might be looking for a feel-good anecdote and land on a convicting example of personal transparency.

Walt Larimore is nothing if not a storyteller. As a friend of many years, he's regaled me (and a handful of fellow writers in a local accountability group) with all manner of tales. And it's clear he loves telling these as much as we enjoy hearing them.

But Dr. Walt is also self-effacing and brutally honest about his own humanity—despite all the accolades that pepper his exhaustive résumé. He was not always the best husband, having to face—and fix—the reality that he allowed his work to interfere with both his spiritual life and his home life.

You couldn't tell that from his active faith and nearly half-century marriage today, but his openness about his early failures seasons this book with a sobering reality.

You'll love it but beware: it's more than fun, homespun stories of small-town medicine. You may see yourself in its mirror; yet trust me, you'll be the better for it in the end.

Jerry B. Jenkins, #1 *New York Times*
bestselling novelist and biographer

PART ONE

1

Near Death

BETH DASHED INTO MY OFFICE. "Dr. Larimore, I need you in the treatment room. Now!"

I threw down the chart I was reading and followed my nurse down the hall and into the procedure room. Patty was placing a blood pressure cuff on a distinguished-looking gentleman with gray hair and a tanned face, but he was critically ill—not fully alert, ashen, and with a cold, clammy forehead.

As I examined him, Beth gave some history. "His name is Dan Autrey. He has a cabin above the Nantahala River. He was working in his yard, clearing some brush, when a swarm of yellowjackets attacked him. His wife said he immediately welted up and itched all over. She gave him two 25-milligram Benadryl capsules and drove him here as fast as she could."

Patty finished taking his vital signs. "Blood pressure only 60 systolic!" she exclaimed. It was abnormally low. "Pulse is 120 and thready. Respirations 32. Pulse ox 88 percent."

All were abnormal. I was sure he was heading into anaphylactic shock from a severe reaction to the venom. Beth pointed to the intubation kit as if to ask if we might need it should his breathing fail. "Let's be prepared; however, get him on oxygen via nasal cannula at two liters a minute." Beth nodded.

"Patty," I barked, "let's get an IV started. Lactated ringers wide open. Beth, get an EpiPen and give one dose IM, stat."

Both of my nurses jumped into action. I turned my attention to the patient. "Mr. Autrey, can you hear me?"

He nodded.

"Mr. Autrey, can you say anything?"

He tried, but he could only whisper. I could not understand his words. I was sure the venom was affecting his vocal cords.

"Beth will give you a shot. It should help."

He nodded again.

Although reactions to insect stings were common in the mountains, the more severe variety, such as this one, was, fortunately, rare. I said a silent prayer the treatment would work quickly.

I admired how well Patty and Beth performed together under pressure. They had worked together in the hospital ER, and it fostered their magnificent teamwork. Beth took the cover off the epinephrine syringe, wiped Dan's skin with an alcohol swab, and then plunged the needle into his right thigh muscle.

I stood back, anxiously waiting for his response, which happened within just a minute or two. His color improved, and his breathing slowed down. He blinked his eyes a few times, and I nodded to Patty to retake his vital signs.

"Blood pressure's up to 90 over 60, pulse 90, respirations 22."

I felt his forehead. It was warmer. "Feeling better?" I asked.

He smiled. "I am."

It was my turn to smile.

"Do you mind if his wife comes back to sit with him?" Beth asked. "She's in the waiting room."

"It's up to Mr. Autrey."

"Just call me Dan," he said. "If Boots can come back, that would be great."

I turned to Beth. "Let's give him another 50 milligrams of oral Benadryl and an injection of 10 milligrams of dexamethasone." Beth nodded, and I explained to Dan: "Benadryl is an antihistamine, and the shot is a steroid. Both will help keep your reaction to the venom at bay. Since you're better, I'm going to see another patient or two, and then I'll be back in to check on you."

When I returned to the treatment room, Dan was sitting up on the procedure table. He no longer looked deathly ill. At his side, holding his hand, was a beautiful woman who appeared to be younger. They were both gazing out the window.

My office sat on the top of a hill overlooking Bryson City, North Carolina, her nine hundred citizens, two stoplights, and thirty-eight Baptist churches, as well as a half-dozen churches of other denominations. To the north was a mesmerizing view up Deep Creek Valley into the heart of Great Smoky Mountains National Park with mile after mile of one distant peak after another, all sporting petticoats of wispy clouds that looked like puffs of smoke—thus the origin of the term *Smoky Mountains*. The setting was spectacular. I never grew tired of admiring the astonishing panorama.

After I introduced myself, she replied, "I'm Boots Autrey."

"Where are you from?" I was sure they weren't from Swain County, and Floridians inhabited—some locals said *infested*—the Autreys' development and a few other small neighborhoods in the Bryson City area.

"We're from a small town in Central Florida called *Kissimmee*. It's near Disney World. We come up here off and on during the year."

"My wife, Barb, and I honeymooned at Disney World."

This comment seemed to spark Boots's interest. "Did you like it?"

"We did. We thought it was a great place to . . . er . . . visit!"

She looked at me. "It's also a great place to live. Why don't you come to practice in our small town? We need more family doctors. And I can tell you, you'd have *no* problem building a practice down there."

"Tell you what," I said, smiling. "If the Lord ever leads us away from this little piece of heaven, I'll give you all a call."

"It's a deal!" Boots responded.

"Here's a prescription for an antihistamine for Dan to take over the next three days and another for an epinephrine pen to keep at the house. I'll have Beth give you instructions on how and when to use it."

After they left, Beth breathed a sigh of relief. "What a dramatic way to start the day! But you did good, Dr. Larimore." That was how the local nurses would compliment a doctor—and high praise for one just starting practice.

I thought, *What if I had not done "good"? What if Dan had not made it? It would have been terrible PR. Everyone knew the local gossip mills in small towns could work for or against you.*

A wiser voice inside chided, *But how can you think only of yourself? This is* not *about your reputation! It's about serving others the best way possible, and you just did that in spades. Well done.*

Part of me felt confident, competent, and capable—the part that thought I was a moral man, a helpful husband, a fine father, and a decent doctor. But another part of me was full of self-doubt and insecurity. The arguments between my two parts always produced internal strife, turning my soul into their personal battlefield. They never agreed to a truce; both refused to raise a white flag or declare a cease-fire. The battle was ever ongoing.

I tried to keep the positive part and banish the negative, but both stayed; one on each shoulder, battling and bickering. One reminded me, *Do you remember what your grandfather used to say? It's never wrong to do what's right!* The other countered, *Don't be impractical. Doing what's right is almost always the more difficult road. Take it easy on yourself!*

It reminded me of how the apostle Paul described his relentless battle. I took some comfort in knowing he wrestled with these same internal voices. "If the power of sin within me keeps sabotaging my best intentions, I obviously need help! I realize that I don't have what it takes. . . . Something has gone wrong deep within me and gets the better of me every time."[1] Then his stronger side said, "I can do all things through Christ who strengthens me."[2] I just needed to depend more upon Yahweh and less on my way.

———

A few weeks later, Dan and Boots showed their appreciation for my staff and me by hosting a dinner at one of the more lovely restaurants in town. As we entered the historic Fryemont Inn, music from the 1940s filled the grand dining room. Wide maple plank flooring original to the 1923 building creaked pleasantly under our feet while large dark chestnut timbers supported the vaulted ceiling. In front of an enormous stone fireplace was a massive table, dressed with a white tablecloth, flatware, and bouquets of colorful flowers separated by scented candles. A smorgasbord of delightful sensations accompanied the warmth of the room—the welcoming fragrance and sounds of a crackling fireplace mingled with the delicious, yeasty, sweet smell of hot, buttered, and freshly baked cathead biscuits piled high on the table.

As we gathered, a tall, debonair man walked in with Dan and Boots and introduced himself. "I'm Kevin Cole. I'm chairman of the Board of Trustees of Humana Hospital Kissimmee. I am up here on vacation with my kids, traveling around the Smokies in an RV. Boots told me how you saved Dan's life."

Before I could object, he continued, "So I asked for permission to drop by and introduce myself. Our hospital board is looking for a few excellent family physicians to come to Kissimmee. If you are ever in the mood to move to one of the most perfect small towns in America, I'm the one who can make it happen." He extolled the virtues of the hospital and community in Central Florida and ended by saying he would fund our meal from the hospital's recruiting budget.

My sinister side thought, *Floridians! They come up here in the good weather, buy up our land, and run up our prices. Then they leave in* winter. *And they don't know how to drive on mountain roads. Nothing worse than needing to get somewhere and getting stuck behind a Floridian!* From my other shoulder, another voice reminded me, *Kind words are like honey—sweet to the soul and healthy for the body,*[3] so I thanked him for his generosity.

"I'd love to stay," he added, "but the kids are in the RV eager for more adventure. I hope to see you in Kissimmee."

I doubted we would ever meet again.

During dessert, Boots leaned over to Barb and me and whispered, "You all really do need to consider our hometown. Kissimmee is not too far from Orlando. It's small, although larger than Bryson City, and has incredible people, hearty congregations, and exemplary schools. Descendants of pioneers inhabit our county. They're wonderful salt-of-the-earth kinda folks. We'd love to have more family doctors there. I hope you'll consider it. We'd cover your expenses to relocate and set up a practice! And since Dan once owned the Ford dealership, you'd never lack for suitable transportation. How about it?"

Barb and I smiled at each other. It was our first experience with what we learned was Boots's renowned persuasive charms. "It pleases me you'd want us there. But living in the Smoky Mountains is a joy. We love the people, the natural environment, the clean air and water, our church, and our new practice."

Boots continued, "There's stunningly beautiful country down in Osceola County. Large lakes with big ole bass and great fishing. Oak trees and Spanish moss. No snow or ice. A wonderful place to raise a family and build a career. You'd love it!"

"We look forward to raising our daughter, Kate"—I reached over to touch Barb's bulging tummy—"and her sibling here in western North Carolina. It's heaven for us."

Boots smiled and patted my arm. "Well, I can understand. There are many reasons tourists visit in the warmer months. But if the dreary winters and endless days without sunshine get to you, you'd be welcome in Osceola County. Our weather is gorgeous all year!"

I cocked my head at her. "Do you work for the Chamber of Commerce down there?"

Dan laughed. "She should, Dr. Larimore. She should!"

Boots chuckled as I thought, *Florida is the* last *place I'd want to live!* My other side countered, *Are you sure? Could those be what they call famous last words? As the mountain folk say, "Don't sell the hide before you shoot the bear."*

2

First Day

DAWN WAS BREAKING as I sat under a massive southern live oak tree. Barb and the kids were still fast asleep as I breathed in the scents from the honeysuckles planted around the deck of our rental house and the exquisite bouquet of my first cup of freshly ground coffee. Looking at my watch, I quickly swigged the last sip of coffee before dashing out the door to drive to the hospital. I remembered our over-six-hundred-mile move from Bryson City to Kissimmee in late 1985, just four years after meeting the Autreys. The circumstances leading to our departure from North Carolina had been agonizing and arduous after learning about the abuse of our children by someone we trusted.

Although only in our early thirties, we had wondered if we had the wherewithal to start over again. Nevertheless, Dan and Boots not only made it happen but also were there to comfort Barb and me every step of the way and in more ways than we could count during our traumatic transition. Besides serving with Kevin Cole on the committee that recruited us, they were there to help smooth the stress and strain of moving to a new community with two young children: six-year-old Kate and three-year-old Scott. They helped us find and move into a small, comfortable rental home in which we lived for six months while sizing up the various areas where we could buy a home.

Dan introduced me to the Rotary Club (where Kevin served as president), the Chamber of Commerce, the Silver Spurs Riding Club (which hosted Kissimmee's twice-a-year rodeo), and many of his friends. Boots made sure Barb met folks and knew of the various church and Bible study options. They honored me beyond measure by becoming two of my very first patients. I always enjoyed our professional and social visits.

I hopped in my old rusty-brown GMC pickup truck. Both it and my marriage had begun life the same year—1973. It had been my daddy's, and I loved that old truck. It was a short, three-mile-and-one-traffic-light commute to my first day at Humana Hospital Kissimmee. It had been founded as Osceola General Hospital in 1933 by a Canadian, Wilson Lancaster, MD.

As I approached the doctors' parking lot, my new partner, John Hartman, MD, was waiting at the gate. He waved to me and then placed a card over a sensor. The arm rose, and he showed me where to park. Truth be told, my old truck looked humble against the array of expensive, brand-spanking-new cars. The doctors were doing *very* well.

John scowled as the parking gate arm remained up. "It should close automatically. Guess I'll report that," he grumbled. He turned to give me a warm hug. As we walked toward the ER entrance, John commented, "It's been seven years since I greeted you this same way at Durham County General Hospital. Gosh, it seems so long ago."

During my internship at Duke, in Durham, North Carolina, John had been my senior resident and helped orient me at the hospital and in becoming a doctor. Leaving residency two years before me, John served with the navy, teaching in a family medicine residency at the Pensacola Naval Air Station. Then he and Cleta, his wife, and their three young daughters had moved to Kissimmee to begin practice, setting up three years before we arrived.

We approached the ER door, where a doctor was having a smoke break. "Ken, this is my new partner, Walt Larimore. Walt, this is Ken Byerly, one of the best ER docs around." We shook hands and went inside for a whirlwind tour.

Jim Shanks, the six-foot, six-inch, handsome and well-dressed hospital administrator, joined us. Even though the hospital had only eighty beds and a six-bed ICU, it looked enormous compared to the hospital in Bryson City. The pediatric wing, nursery, and maternity care suites were modern and well-appointed. We passed the front desk, and after meeting the pink ladies—volunteers for the day—turned to meet the hospital switchboard operator.

"Dolly, meet our newest doctor."

Dolly stood and flashed a gleaming smile. "Dr. John has said some nice things about you. Welcome."

Her warm greeting was with a voice made for radio. *No wonder she's the operator,* I thought. She turned to answer an incoming call as Jim excused himself. John and I went to the doctors' lounge to complete paperwork and take a staff photo for my ID card.

As we were drinking our coffee, I heard Dolly's voice over the intercom. "Ladies and gentlemen, would the person who parked the old brown GMC pickup truck in the doctors' parking lot move it at once or the police will ticket and tow it." As my face flushed and John laughed, she repeated the message.

"Why don't you go take care of that, Walt," John said. "Dolly can find me when you're done."

In the parking lot, a police officer was talking to a physician in surgical scrubs and a white coat. "I think I'm the offender you're looking for, gentlemen."

"I'm Officer Gib Michaels," the policeman said. "Is this your truck?"

I nodded.

"This lot is for doctors only. If you move it to the visitors' lot, I won't have to ticket you."

"I *am* a doctor."

Before I could explain, the physician interrupted. "I'm Dr. Gonzales. I know *all* the doctors, but I don't know you!"

"He's mine!" a voice behind us shouted. We all turned to see Jim Shanks striding toward us. "Pete, Gib, this is our newest doctor. You guys can't haul him off to jail. We need him."

The men chuckled.

"He's here today completing all the forms and procedures."

"Well, that explains why you don't have a parking sticker," Dr. Gonzales said.

"Walt, Officer Michaels is one of Kissimmee's finest," Jim explained. "When he was an athlete at Osceola High not too very long ago, he was one of the best in the state."

Gib blushed and looked down.

"Dr. Pete Gonzales is our chief of staff and one of the best surgeons around. He also is the head physician for our ER, the EMTs, as well as the police and fire departments."

Pete turned to the officer. "Officer Michaels, sorry for the trouble. We'll take it from here."

"No trouble at all, Dr. Gonzales." Gib turned and shook my hand. "Welcome to Kissimmee, Doctor. I look forward to working with you."

"Pete, you mind walking Walt in?" Jim asked. "I've got to run and meet a family."

Pete nodded. As we walked back into the hospital, Pete apologized.

"Not a problem." I asked about his background. He was a first-generation Filipino American, a general surgeon, a US Army Reserve colonel, and a decorated Vietnam MASH surgeon. He mentioned how he admired and enjoyed working with Dr. Hartman and had been looking forward to meeting me.

"John told me you were instrumental in his getting his hospital privileges," I said.

"That's true, but not just me. Jim Shanks and Kevin Cole also went to bat for you guys in front of the hospital board of directors and before the medical staff. In the past, we've only had specialists and GPs here. John and two other young doctors were the first residency-trained, board-certified family physicians who applied for privileges. Most of our doctors have not worked with FPs. I wasn't surprised that a few of the Ob-Gyns weren't sure they wanted FPs delivering babies. None of the pediatricians were open to your ilk being in what they saw as *their* nursery or pediatric wing. And don't get me started on the ICU doctors. I thought they would have heart attacks when they learned FPs wanted to take care of patients in *their* ICU. Thank goodness we have that straightened out." After looking up and down the hall, he leaned toward me and whispered, "But don't screw it up. I spent a lot of political capital fighting for those guys, and by extension, you. I can't afford for you to make some silly mistake. So I have some advice for you."

"I'm listening."

"I'd suggest being liberal getting consults for a while. That way, you get to know the subspecialists, and they'll get used to you. I've reviewed your recommendations from residency and Bryson City. I've called and talked to the folks you've worked with over the last few years. They speak highly of you."

He took a half step back and looked up at me over crossed arms. "I want to be able to do the same. Understand?"

I nodded.

"There's one other item I need to broach with you. It's sensitive. May I?"

"Of course," I said, wondering what might be next.

"It's that truck of yours. As you likely noticed, the doctors here don't drive trucks. Wranglers and ranchers do. Farmers and cowboys do. Doctors do *not*. There is a professional image we need to uphold and maintain. Is that understood?"

I was dumbfounded and speechless. I loved my truck!

"My brother owns a car dealership in Orlando. I'll call him and get a Mercedes delivered to you later today or tomorrow. Knowing you're just starting a practice, it will be pre-owned. But it will be in perfect condition. Then, once you're making a decent income, he'll get a brand-new leased one for you each year. Or he can get you two if your wife needs one. She doesn't drive a truck, also, does she?"

I chuckled. "No, sir. She most definitely does *not*."

"What color do you want?"

I had no idea. "Blue," was all I could think to say. It was my favorite color.

"Let's go get a cup of coffee, and then I'll show you *my* surgical suites."

"Are you the only surgeon?"

Pete's eyebrows furrowed. "Of course not," he said, leaning toward me, "but I am the best."

As I was to learn over time, this was *not* bragging, but stating a fact.[1]

3

Gonna Like Him

AFTER FINISHING MY TOUR with Dr. Gonzales, I caught up with John on the medical wing, and we made rounds together. He introduced me to his patients, now *our* patients, the staff, and the nurses, including Judy Simpson, who was the charge nurse for the shift. A perky, outgoing blonde, she observed, "Dr. Larimore, you look *too* young to be a doctor. Are you still in college?"

People often kidded me about my boyish looks, but not usually at a first meeting. I replied, "My grandchildren say the same thing."

Judy looked confused. "You have grandchildren?"

I shook my head. "Just kidding," I said as we all laughed.

John commented, "Judy, when are you coming to work with me at my office?" He looked at me. "I've been trying to hire her as my nurse since I got here. She's considering it."

"Only if she turns me down," said a gruff voice behind us.

We turned to see a tall, stocky Hispanic man in surgical scrubs with a five o'clock shadow, and it was still midmorning. "You must be the new guy." He stuck out his large hand. "I'm Frank Crespo, the best urologist you'll ever meet."

"He's the best one here in Kissimmee," John said.

Crespo let out a booming laugh. "Because I'm the *only* one in town. Gotta go," he said as he turned. "The OR beckons."

"Humble, eh?" I noted.

"Not in the slightest," John replied.

Judy added, "If you bought him for what he was worth and sold him for what he thought he was worth, you'd make a fortune. He's said to be the richest doctor in the community. Heck, his automobile costs more than most people's houses, his monthly mortgage is more than our annual ones combined, and he seems to take great pride in showing off his many expensive possessions."

John laughed. "Well, he's brash, arrogant, cocky, flashy, flamboyant, and worldly. And he's self-assured, that's for sure, but he's a fabulous urologist, a great technician in the OR, and a good friend."

Judy leaned toward us. "Dr. Hartman, maybe I will consider coming over to the office and chatting with you. Shift work at the hospital is getting old—like me!"

"You don't look like you've had a birthday in . . . ten years!" John exclaimed.

"Flattery will get you everywhere," she said, laughing, as she turned back to her work. "And you've got patients to see."

John oriented me to the charting system and some clinical processes. At one nurses' station, Mr. Shanks walked in and greeted each of the nurses and ward clerks by name, inquiring about work and their families. As he was walking out, he stopped by the doctors' charting area.

"I was hoping to find you guys as I practiced my ambulatory management," he said, smiling.

"What's that?" I asked. "I've never heard the term."

He nodded. "I manage by walking around. Most hospital administrators never leave their executive suite. They are too aloof or arrogant to do so. I love my staff; I love visiting with them at least once each shift."

"Sometimes when I'm here at night, Jim will be here visiting with his staff," John said.

"It allows me to sense the pulse of my hospital and people, and it allows me to address *their* issues and concerns long before they become *my* problems."

I remembered a night on call during my first month as a family medicine resident at Duke. We had an abnormally high number of admissions. My stress and anxiety level were sky-high as it was hard enough learning how to be a doctor, how to navigate in a new hospital and use a new medical record system, where things were located, and many new names and faces—and to keep so many spinning plates from crashing to the floor. On top of all this, I was on my fourth admission, with several waiting to be seen. A hand rested on my shoulder, and a reassuring voice said, "I've heard you guys were getting creamed. How can I help?" It was my residency director, Terry Kane, MD. He had left the nurses a message to call him if any of his interns got too busy or overwhelmed so that he could come in and help. My admiration for his care and caring was enormous.

When Barb and I had interviewed at Duke, John and Cleta had shown us around. When they introduced us to Terry, John had said, "You're gonna really like him."

I could understand how Jim's staff must have felt when he did the same for them.

"Hey, John," Jim said. "I'd like to make a recording that we could use in our radio advertising to let people know more about family docs. Would that be okay?"

"I'd be happy to," John replied.

Jim reached into his coat pocket and pulled out a small voice recorder. "Is now okay?"

John nodded, so Jim turned on the recorder and spoke into it. "I'm here with John R. Hartman, MD, one of Kissimmee's residency-trained and board-certified family physicians. Dr. Hartman, in a sentence or two, why are you a family physician?"

John didn't even hesitate. "For me, this was the only pathway. I wanted to be a physician who cares for the family. I love family medicine because of its breadth. Every day is different. It is nice to care for patients of all ages and to be able to tell them that I have a 90–95 percent chance of being able to help them. And if I can't, I'll help them find the care they need. I get great joy being the doctor who can care for the whole person and their entire family."

Jim smiled. "One more question, if I may. Here at the hospital, the feds foist more and more regulations on us, making my life more difficult every year. Does the government make it harder for physicians also?"

"It certainly does!" John exclaimed. "But one thing they can't steal is the joy of practicing family medicine. It's a unique opportunity to help people, their families, and the community. The gleam in a patient's eyes or their smile at the end of the encounter is a more valuable payment to me than the check they write when they leave. My reward is seeing the thanks in their eyes."

Jim smiled and clicked off the recorder. "That was perfect. Now I just need to write some copy to go along with this in the newspaper."

"Oh," I said. "I might have something." I pulled out my wallet. "My wife found this somewhere while we were in Bryson City. Maybe it would work." I unfolded a small piece of paper and handed it to him.

Jim read, "If it creaks, cramps, cries, eats, stings, smarts, swells, twists, twinges, burps, burns, aches, sticks, twitches, crumbles, or hurts, we've got just the doctor for you."[1] He smiled. "This is perfect. Do you know the source?"

I shook my head.

"I'm gonna use it. I'll just add, 'Choose one of our board-certified, residency-trained family physicians. They provide primary care and primary caring for you and your entire family."

"It's perfect," John said. "I like it."

"Me too," I added.

"Sounds good. I think it's great. Well, I need to shove off. Welcome, Dr. Larimore."

As Jim strode down the hall, John commented, "He loves his people and *most* of his doctors."

Judy walked by and added, "That's just one of the many reasons we love that man so much. You're gonna really like him too."[2]

4

Different Drummers

THE NEXT DAY, John and I began a habit that would continue for a decade and a half. At about 10:00 a.m. each office day, our office manager, Susan Mongillo, would herd us to the break room. We'd have coffee and share a joke or two and something about our family lives or interesting patients. Then we'd have a short prayer. Rarely did I not learn something from this remarkable man. He was intensely tuned to a different channel in life and had a unique focus—different from most physicians.

John's center point and north star were the things of the Lord. Many physicians prioritize pleasures, possessions, and power. Some who have religious or spiritual tendencies consider godly goals as an add-on to life. But John chose a narrower path. He never missed daily Mass and would tell me, "It's my time to recenter on what's important in the creation and the cosmos." He was an avid student of Scripture. In short, his life was God-centered.

As a young man, John wanted to become a priest—at least until he met and married Cleta. After college, he began a career as an electrical engineer but sensed a call to become a family physician. In Kissimmee, he built a small, successful, patient-centered, and

God-focused practice. He would often say, "I like to practice by *the* Book—the Word of God and its principles." To me, my family, and my patients' eternal benefit, John invited me to join him on a marvelous professional and personal journey together.

When patients and people in our community saw John put God and church ahead of personal gain and pleasure, they sometimes said, "He marches to the beat of a different drummer!"

He would respond, "So be it. I can't wait to introduce them to the drummer."

One morning, when I stepped out of a patient room, Susan was waiting for me in the hallway. "I need to show you something." She nodded her head for me to follow. We exited through the back door of the office and there, sitting next to my daddy's truck, was a shiny, blue Mercedes Benz sedan.

A short, plumpish Filipino man introduced himself as Pete's brother and handed me the keys. "These are for you."

"Do I need to sign anything?"

"No, sir. Pete and my people took care of everything—license, title, plates, registration, and insurance. It's yours for a ninety-day trial. No charge, no commitment. If for any reason you don't like it, just call me, and we can take it back or trade it in for another."

After we all went on a test drive, Pete's brother left. As Susan and I walked back into the office, she explained, "I think Dr. Gonzales does this with all the new docs. What 'cha gonna do? Keep it?"

I chuckled. "Before today I had never driven, much less owned, an expensive automobile. Although I must admit, it drove like a dream."

"It was plush and comfortable and amazing," Susan said.

I nodded. "But I don't think it's me."

"Why not?" she asked as we entered the staff lounge and poured cups of coffee.

"I grew up in a family with simple tastes. We had no luxuries. My parents taught my three brothers and me to 'dress down' and not to show off. We weren't wealthy financially, but we were healthy, happy, and well cared for. Above all else, we boys knew our parents loved us. Our mom and dad's priorities were faith, family, and friends. Our lack of money growing up made us depend on each other, appreciate and respect each other, and support and fight for one another. We had everything that counted. That's an upbringing from which I don't think I'll escape—nor do I want to."

"So I guess you're not going to keep it, eh?"

"Nope. But it might be nice to drive for a few days."

She smiled. "Don't blame you."

"Did Dr. Gonzales get one for Dr. John?"

Susan nodded. "Of course, but he didn't keep his either. I think you two are cut from the same cloth."

What a nice compliment, one side of me said. *Just wait till she gets to know the real you*, said the other. That one reminded me of my grandfather, who always asked, "Is your juice worth the squeeze?" I could only hope mine was!

With apologies to Pete and his brother, I returned the vehicle two weeks later. I prized and drove my dad's truck for the next fifteen years. Kate and Scott learned to drive in that trusty rust bucket. When Scott, as a teenager, drove that junker around town, everyone knew it was him. In fact, he couldn't go anywhere without being recognized. I'd like to think it kept him out of a lot of temptation and trouble.

At 2:00 a.m. one morning, racing to the hospital to deliver a baby, I rolled through a stop sign without coming to a complete stop. I didn't see Officer Michaels in his police car across the street, waiting to catch the frequent speeders or stop-sign runners who endangered that intersection. By now, he knew my truck. I began to slow down to pull off the road, when he popped out of his car, a gleaming smile unfolding, and waved me on.

Although he let my infraction slide, someone else did not.

That week John invited me to attend Rotary Club with him as a visitor. During the meeting, it delighted Chief Frank Ross of the Kissimmee Police Department to mention what happened that week, and club president, Kevin Cole, immediately fined me the excessive amount of five dollars for the transgression.

"You can't fine him!" John protested.

"Why not?" Kevin asked.

"He's not a member!"

"Then, I'll fine you!" Kevin proclaimed.

The entire room guffawed and applauded. I felt welcome and even more so when John happily walked up front to pay for my transgression.

"Welcome to the team," he said, smiling, as he returned. "I guess this officially makes us partners in the eyes of these old-timers. And that's a good thing, trust me!"

Henry David Thoreau wrote, "If a man does not keep pace with his companions, perhaps it is because he hears a different drummer. Let him step to the music which he hears, however measured or far away."[1] Early on in our practice, it pleased me to realize that John and I were going to dance to the same tune together.

5

Back to Nature

ALTHOUGH KISSIMMEE IS ONLY about fifteen miles as the crow flies from Disney World, the drive from the world-famous theme park to our new hometown was like traveling into the rural countryside during another time in history. I always felt as if I were passing through an invisible but almost palpable curtain.

On one side were the swank, modern resorts, ubiquitous tourist shops, copious chain restaurants, and endless traffic jams. The other had lonely, two-lane rural asphalt, gravel, and dirt roads cloaked by massive, moss-covered oak trees bordering endless acres of orange groves and pastures. Innumerable snowy and cow egrets surrounded peacefully grazing cattle. Herds of small white-tail deer would step around wild turkeys as they skirted small cypress hollows and marshes.

In many of the idyllic fields, raucous sandhill cranes, standing four to five feet tall, looked regal with their long, thin legs and necks. In most of North America, they are migratory, but in this paradise, the Florida sandhill cranes stay all year.

Their cheeks are white, and their foreheads display a bright red patch, one of their most noticeable features. The males put on comical dancing displays and flap their impressive five- to six-foot wingspans while bowing, running, and jumping several feet into the air. Often, they throw a stick or some grass into the air to impress nearby females and scare away younger males. Once a pair of sandhills mate, they remain together for life.

Soaring bald eagles, ospreys, and turkey vultures, all hunting for their next meal, eyed the amusing dancers from on high. I could roll down my truck windows and enjoy the light scents of hay, grass, and pine trees. The countryside created ever-changing but contenting olfactory sensations.

The population of Kissimmee numbered just over fifteen thousand folks, many of whom, like the Autreys, counted themselves as multigenerational residents. The town sat near one of the largest lakes in Florida, Lake Tohopekaliga, often called Lake Toho. "Some old-timers often say *Tohopekaliga* means 'sleeping tiger,' referring to the lake's propensity to flood the surrounding land before the installation of flood-control canals in the 1960s," Dan told me. "Others say it's a native name meaning 'we will gather here.'"

"Where does the name *Kissimmee* come from?" I asked.

"Some say it means 'a place where mulberries grow.' Others say it refers to this area as being the headwaters of the Kissimmee River. Most say the name was derived from the ancient Indian term *Cacema*."

Dan had to teach me how to pronounce Kissimmee. He said, "It's ka-SIM-me, with the emphasis on the middle." Then laughing, he added, "But at night, just after our prayers, Boots and I always pronounce it KISS-a-me, and then we do, with an emphasis on the lips!"

As for the name of the lake, Dan pronounced it *Ta-hoe-pa-ka-like-ah*. "Most folks just call it Lake Toho, but bass fishermen call it 'one of the best bass lakes in the world.' In fact, where Shingle Creek flows into the lake, someone caught a twenty-four-pound, twelve-ounce largemouth bass. They said it measured over thirty-nine inches long and thirty inches around. Can you believe that?"

I wasn't sure I did, but a local bass fishing guide clarified the monster fish was netted during an electroshock survey in 1974. Another guide told me of local fishers who had caught even bigger bass but who did not take the time or trouble to get them registered for the record books. The lake holds many official records, with the most famous being the heftiest five-bass limit in history—forty-five pounds and two ounces.[1]

Sunrises astounded us as the bright yellow-orange orb slowly rose above the mist-shrouded meadows. But the sunsets repeatedly stunned us—out-of-control, insanely beautiful, and bursting with vivid colors.

One evening we drove from our temporary rental home to a lakeside park. Sitting by Lake Toho, a gentle wind blowing, we watched Kate and Scott play together as the sky exploded into a kaleidoscope of colors. I held Barb close, whispering, "It's awesome."

She hugged me. "I'm not sure this is word for word, but 'The heavens declare the glory of God; the skies proclaim the work of his hands.'[2] No wonder people whisper, 'Oh, my God!' whenever they see some awesome wonder of nature."

"It's like God is engraving his autograph into each sunset."

"What name do you think he uses?" she asked.

"He just writes, 'I am.'"

We never tired of admiring them—often in astonishment and even reverence—experiencing a joy that radiated from outside ourselves. In moments like this, we forgot both our troubles and ourselves—soaking in the brilliance and splendor.

I realized these special occasions were not ones of self-satisfaction but self-forgetfulness. Times in which I overflowed with admiration for the Creator and his creation—appreciative of a magnificent joy that can only come from outside ourselves. During one of these marvelous sunsets, I realized God created me—and each of us—to both enjoy him and reflect his glory in every sphere of our lives.

Thunderstorms could blow in at only a moment's notice, with howling winds, driving rain, and fierce lightning. As we watched one approach from the southwest, a wall of monsoon-like rain raced toward us across the lake; we could smell the intensifying sweet ozone.

We sat and waited until the very last moment before gathering our kids and blankets and sprinting to the car, laughing all the way and arriving with seconds to spare.

At night, there were so few city lights that the sky glistened with stars, constellations, and the shimmering of the Milky Way. Frogs, crickets, and katydids provided a symphonic overture to nature's spectacular planetarium. I would gaze at the spectacle and hum the old hymn:

> This is my Father's world,
> And to my listening ears
> All nature sings, and round me rings
> The music of the spheres.[3]

That the Creator did this for each of us to see was a delightful thought. That he had moved us here was reassuring and comforting. Our painful past began to melt away.[4]

6

Cowboy Country

ONE EVENING DAN AUTREY drove me around the lake and out King's Highway, turning off to meander down an almost-one-mile-long dirt road. "I want to show you the lake from another angle. This is the ranch of my older sister, Connie, and her husband. His given name is Edward Louis, but everyone calls him *Geech*. He served as the best man at my wedding, and like sis and me, he is a third-generation Osceolean. He and his brothers inherited over twenty-five thousand acres of Osceola County ranch land on which they all were born and raised. Suspect they'll all die here; that's if the tourists don't run 'em off. They've wanted to meet you."

I slowly inhaled the earthy, humid fragrance of the countryside. We passed man-made canals that drained the former swampland and created lush pastures occupied by grazing Brahman and Angus cattle. The early evening air was moist and muggy, and the gentle wind wafting through Dan's truck enveloped and hugged me. From my earliest camping days as a Boy Scout, I had always loved getting away from the city. The more rural it was, the more at home I felt.

"By nature and nurture," Dan continued, "ranching is their way of life. The Partins are a breed of folk most people don't have a clue still exists today: the old-time Florida cowboy. They've adhered to a lifestyle and a strength of character that has survived virtually unchanged for centuries. I'm right proud to call 'em family." Dan laughed and added, "But don't you dare tell 'em I said so!"

We drove up to a small brick ranch home and parked. "Geech and Connie have been married for nearly fifty years. They built this house themselves with salvaged antique bricks they hauled on a horse-drawn wagon from an abandoned and tumbledown sugar mill erected in the 1880s between here and St. Cloud."

The house was situated next to a large red barn on the east shore of Lake Toho across from downtown. Palm trees at the edge of the water gently swayed in the evening breeze. We found the older couple sharing a glass of iced tea on their back porch. They rose to greet us.

Geech had a round face, tanned and deeply creased by years of sun and weather extremes. His nose ridge was crooked, likely from past trauma of various kinds. He was short and stocky and well-muscled. He tipped his Stetson and stuck out his calloused hand in greeting. Although his fingers were twisted, gnarly, and ravaged by arthritis and many accidents from cowboying, his grip remained strong and firm. Like all ranchers, he looked you straight in the eye when he shook your hand. I felt he was sizing me up and it turned out he was!

Connie was average height and, given her age, moved with surprising gracefulness. Her silver hair crowned a thin face, wrinkled as much from laughter as from ranch living. Her radiant smile exuded welcome. She wore glasses, but one quickly got the idea she could see into your heart. "Nice to meet you, Dr. Larimore. You're welcome here. Will you have a seat and join us a bit?"

As she went into the house to bring out more iced tea, a large bull walked past the porch and bellowed. "That's Wrinkles," Geech proudly boasted. "He's my favorite, and he knows it. Weighs nearly two tons, but he's just a big baby. Follows me around the pastures like a puppy." Geech laughed. How I would grow to love his laughter. It came easily for him. This was his land, and it gave him great pride and comfort.

As Connie poured tea for us, Geech continued. "Florida has the longest history of ranching of any state in the United States," he explained. "The first cattle were brought here by the expeditions of Ponce de León in 1521 and Don Diego de Maldonado in 1540. Some of their stock escaped and survived in the wild. Organized ranching began around St. Augustine in about 1565 when cattle from Spain and Cuba were imported to feed the settlements. In those days, they called the boys who worked cattle *cowmen*, but by the late 1800s, folks referred to them as *cow hunters* because they had to hunt for cattle scattered over the wooded rangelands and swamps during roundups. By the time of my arrival here in Osceola County, we just used the term *cowboy*." He finished his tea and looked over the cattle walking toward the lake. "My family inherited not just the land, but over 450 years of heritage."

"Where'd your family come from? And how many of you were there?"

"The Partin clan arrived in Central Florida from Georgia in the mid-1800s. Daddy was born in Partin Settlement just a bit east of here in 1890. Daddy married Mama—she was a Bass—in 1909. They had five boys and one girl. Me and my brothers and all the sons and grandsons were born within fifteen miles of Kissimmee."

"How about you, Dan?" I asked.

"Of our crew," Dan replied, "I'm the young'un. Geech and Connie were born in 1914, me not until 1921."

Connie laughed. "You just look older than me!"

Dan chuckled. "That's from growing up with three older and bossier sisters. We were all born in Autreyville, Georgia—and, yes, it was named after a relative. Our family moved here when I was three. We all attended Osceola High School, the home of the Kissimmee Kowboys. That's 'Kowboy' with a K, not a C. Back then, the big rivalry was with the St. Cloud Bulldogs from 'bout ten miles to the east. Guess it's still a pretty intense rivalry, although

Kissimmee usually comes out on top. All of my childhood memories are from right here in Osceola County."

"Me too," Geech added. "One of my fondest is that Daddy designed a brand for each of my brothers and me the day we were born. From the time we were old enough to climb on a horse until long after Daddy died in 1974, we all worked side by side virtually every day of the year. We worked together so long that we knew what each other was thinking. Heck, we knew what each other was going to say before he said it. Many a cattle drive forged the unity of our family. We're a close crew."

"I've never asked, and you've never mentioned it," Dan said. "What's your earliest memory as a boy?"

He thought a moment and then smiled. "I was riding the grasslands south of St. Cloud. Back then, this area was as much of a frontier as the wild west had been. It was as rare to see someone out there as I imagine it would be riding the prairies of Wyoming or South Dakota. We could ride for days seeing nothing but big ole pine and cypress forests, deer and ospreys until we located our cattle. In fact, most of Central Florida was open range. We could ride from here to the east coast, 'bout fifty miles east and ninety miles to the south to Lake Okeechobee at the start of the Everglades. No fences anywhere. The big lumber companies and other ranchers let us freely graze our stock on their land." He took a swig of tea, took off his hat, wiped his brow, and then rubbed the cold glass against his forehead. A look of sheer bliss settled across his face, and then he let out another laugh. "Just remembered riding a small mule across a palmetto scrub range when I was a tot— following Daddy, one of my uncles, and my older brother Slim as they rounded up cattle."

"Why a mule?" I asked.

"I was just four or five, and we Partin boys didn't get our own horses until we were six or seven. Also, Daddy felt I was too small to handle a horse. But I didn't mind as long as I could ride the range with the others."

"You rode that mule for a couple of years, didn't you?" Connie said. "What was his name? I forget."

"Jack."

Connie laughed. "I remember now. He was still alive when we were kids. Had mighty long ears and would bite anyone who tried to touch him."

"Jack toughened me up. I loved that little guy. But for me and my brothers, being invited to take part in the cattle drives showed a measure of acceptance as a working cowboy. Nothing made me happier than being able to saddle up and ride out with 'em. We boys were raised out there in cattle camps. I slept better on the ground in a bedroll than I did in any bed. We'd rise before the sun and not settle down until after it set. Lived days and sometimes weeks at a time on coffee, dried beef, beans, and biscuits. It was hard, hard work, but I wouldn't trade it for nothing."

"Geech is a proud cattleman and horseman," Dan said. "He doesn't mind bragging about his family, his ranch, and his native state."

"Doc," Geech said, leaning toward me, "it ain't bragging if'n it's a fact." He settled back, laughing again. "We're in the top ten states in the country producing beef cattle. Heck, we're the largest cattle-producing state east of the Mississippi River, and we have the largest rodeo east of the 'Old Muddy.' Osceola County is one of the biggest ranching counties in the state. The weather can be challenging from time to time. But the cattle and us cowboys, like them palm trees there on our shore, we all kinda flourish in it."

Dan added, "New folks are often heard around here saying, 'Don't like the weather? Wait fifteen minutes.' Most of us old-timers say, 'Don't like the weather? Move!'"

They all laughed. Geech leaned toward me again. "If you like Kissimmee, and if you like us, stay—become one of us. Become, if not a cowboy, at least a local!" He chuckled. "Like I tell my boys, 'Don't ask folks where they're from. If they're from Kissimmee, they'll proudly tell ya so. And if they're not, you don't want to embarrass 'em!" He and Dan laughed hilariously.

As I sipped my tea, I realized that in my short time here, I had come to sense a palpable friction between the old and the new, the insider and the outsider, the town and the country; all accompanied the timeless fluctuations in temperature and temperament. I was going to have to learn to navigate a cool to blistering, humid to oppressive, dry to sticky, and calm to turbulent climate and personalities. We had experienced the same in Bryson City and thought we might escape it here. But I was coming to see this was small-town America, and this would be my family's norm again. Just like the rural Smokies from which we had come, the more quickly we could transition from being newcomers, the better!

"Mr. Partin—"

"Please!" he interrupted. "Just call me Geech."

"Geech, I have a question. How long does it take to become local here in Osceola County?"

He scrunched his sun-weathered face, lifted his old cowboy hat with a calloused hand to wipe his gleaming brow, and growled, "I need to know your grandpappy." He put his hat on and added, "Real good."

I suspected he was right. After saying our goodbyes, Dan drove down the long country road that served as the Partins' driveway. I was lost in my thoughts. The juxtaposition of their old traditions, anchored in faith and family, to the new customs my family was just beginning to create made me feel nervous about how we'd be received, how we'd settle in. I was jealous of what they had yet anxious to set down new roots of my own. Out of the tears and torment of our family tragedy in North Carolina, in which our marriage and our faith had been tested by fire, arose new opportunities—a new family, a new practice, a new community life—all ready to commence.

Dan reached over and put his hand on my shoulder. "You and Barb are gonna do just fine. I know it. You've got each other, and you've got the Lord."

I smiled as the evening coolness drifted through the truck.

"And," he added, "you've set in with one of the best docs around. You've got Boots and me on your side. And, I suspect, Geech and Connie. It bodes for a promising start."

I leaned back as we bumped along the dirt road, the truck headlights illuminating the long road ahead. I was looking forward to starting afresh. *Maybe the pain and tears are finally behind me,* I thought.

Suddenly the truck lurched and forcefully bounced. "Wasn't expecting that!"

Dan laughed. "Never know when you're gonna hit a pothole! Always show up when you least expect 'em."

As my family began to settle into this remarkable environment, Kissimmee became not only our new family home but the laboratory in which the spiritual faith of each member of my family developed and matured at an exponential rate. Just like a child or a plant that seems to "shoot up overnight," my time in the greenhouse—some would say *hothouse*—of rural Central Florida was to be a season in which my proficiency as a physician, my capacity as a husband and father, and my progression as a man of faith would increase. At the same time, I was to experience some severe pruning—some deep potholes. The next few years would change my family and me forever.[1]

PART TWO

7

First Call

JOHN AND I ROTATED night and weekend calls with two other family physicians who had served with John in the navy. The guys were kind enough to let me settle into office practice for a week before having my first night on call.

After dinner, while Barb was putting Scott to bed with a story and prayer time, I was helping Kate into her pajamas. She had been born with cerebral palsy—think of a baby in the womb having a stroke and losing blood supply to part of the brain. It left her with minimal right brain tissue and only about half of her left brain. Yet, through the years, with much love, prayer, intense therapy, and multiple surgeries, Kate could now walk without braces. She was mainstreamed into regular instead of special needs classes at school and proved to be a quick learner, an avid reader, and an excellent student. As I tucked Kate into bed, my beeper vibrated. It was the ER notifying me I had a patient to see ASAP. I kissed everyone goodnight, not knowing how long I would be away from home.

At the stop sign closest to the hospital, I was sure to come to a full stop. As I pulled forward, I saw a blink of headlights from a vehicle in the shadows of a building across the street. The cab lights of the Kissimmee Police cruiser turned on, and Gib's smile beamed as he waved.

Only three cars occupied the doctors' parking lot, but the ER waiting room was overflowing. Ken Byerly was at the doctors' station and stood to greet me. "So sorry to call you in, Walt. A patient of Dr. Hartman's has a deep arm laceration. Normally, I'd just sew it up for you guys and not bother you, but I'm too packed tonight. Do you mind helping me out?"

"Not a problem. Glad to."

"Not me!" boomed a voice behind us. Walking in, dressed in scrubs, sporting a 9:00 p.m. facial shadow and a half-smoked cigarette hanging from his mouth, Frank Crespo wrapped his massive arms around each of our shoulders—Ken on one side, me on the other. "Gotta go to the OR and save lives."

Judy Simpson, serving that night as the ER charge nurse, walked by. "You may be saving lives, Dr. Crespo, but you *cannot* smoke in my emergency room."

Frank muttered, "Mrs. Simpson, I'll smoke any blankety-blank place I want to. Am I right, Dr. Byerly?"

Judy walked over and jerked the cigarette out of Frank's mouth. "Any blankety-blank place except *my* ER, Dr. Crespo." She strode out the back door to dispose of the butt.

"I wouldn't recommend riling up my nurse, Frank," cautioned Ken.

"You should advise her *not* to rile me up. You know I'm Cuban, and I can use voodoo to put some juju on her." He hurried out of the ER, a trail of tobacco smoke and fumes swirling behind him.

"Juju?" I asked.

"I think it's something the Cuban Santería priests or witch doctors do."

"Santería?"

"A religion that developed in Cuba among West African descendants. Some Cubans in South Florida practice it and mix in animal sacrifice and voodoo. At one of our ER conferences, I heard a talk from Dade County's chief deputy medical examiner, who is an expert on Santería. He said the cult is flourishing with thousands practicing it—both black magic and white magic sects—whatever that means."

"I'm not sure I want to find out," I replied.

"Dr. Byerly, our patient in the trauma room is coding!" yelled Judy.

"Need help?" I asked.

"I'll let you know!" Ken said as he raced to the room, and Dolly called the code over the intercom.

After changing into surgical scrubs, I looked over the chart, learning my patient was a teenage boy whose horse had thrown him on the family ranch. His arm smashed against a sharp piece of the metal siding of a shed and cut it to the bone. I went in to see him and meet the family. After introductions, I took off the compression dressing. Although the wound was deep, it was clean, and there were no lacerated nerves, major vessels, or tendons. I'd have to close it in several layers, and it would take a while, but I assured the boy and his family that I expected uncomplicated healing.

Judy stepped out of the trauma room. "The code team has it under control. Can I assist you?"

Together, we numbed and scrubbed the wound before I sewed it closed with over sixty stitches. Judy dressed the wound, while I finished the chart at the doctors' station, ordered tetanus and antibiotic shots, wrote prescriptions for an oral antibiotic and pain medication, and completed instructions for wound care and follow-up.

"I checked on Ken," Judy said. "He and the code team were still working on the patient. They successfully resuscitated him and are stabilizing him before transfer to the ICU."

"Should I offer to help?"

"They're fine, but I need you to see another of Dr. Hartman's patients, if you would." I could tell her request was urgent.

"Sure, what is it?"

"A sweet little girl who put a small ring on a large finger and can't get it off. The finger is swollen and uncomfortable. I think we need to get the ring cutter to remove it."

"The ring or the finger?" I asked, trying not to smile.

Judy gave me an annoyed look as I grabbed the clipboard chart, reviewed it, and walked into the room to introduce myself. The young girl, contrary to her mother's instructions, had placed a pinkie ring on her ring finger. Now, neither the young girl nor her mother could remove the ring despite many frantic attempts. The more they tried to remove it, the more swollen and painful the finger became. By the time they arrived, the girl's situation was desperate—not just physically but also emotionally.

"Don't cut my ring off," the girl pleaded. "It's from my grandma. Please! Please don't cut it!" She dissolved into sobs.

What came to mind was a trick the older doctors in Bryson City taught me. "I don't think I'll have to cut your ring. At least, I'll try not to."

She began to calm down. I asked Judy if there was a roll of string or twine available. There was none. "Any dental floss?"

"I have some dental tape in my purse," she offered. "But for what?"

"Can I use it?"

"Of course."

I explained to the mother and girl my plan, and they agreed to let me try it. The old country-doctor trick was to wrap the floss firmly around the finger, starting at the fingernail and move up toward the knuckle row-by-row, leaving no visible skin between each circle. It took several moments and yards of the floss until the digit looked mummified. As I wrapped, the built-up swelling passed under the ring and up into the hand. The theory was that the compression would allow the ring to slide over the sore but "skinny" finger.

The trick worked, to the delight of Judy, the mother, her daughter, and even me. Soon the precious ring was past the knuckle and off the finger. After unrolling the floss, the postprocedure exam showed the finger's circulation and sensation were normal. I assured the mom that the dental floss impression in the skin would soon disappear.

I stepped out of the cubicle and saw Ken coming out from another one.

"How'd it go?" I asked.

"Got him off to the ICU. One of our cardiologists is taking care of him. I think he'll make it, but it was nip and tuck there for a bit. Thanks for seeing those patients."

"Not a problem. It turns out they both were patients of Dr. Hartman's. I had to use an old country-doctor trick on one."

After I explained what I had done, Ken asked, "Well, do you have any old country-doc tricks for starting an IV on a dehydrated patient? Judy and I can't get one started, so I have her setting up for me to do a central line."

I knew that meant Ken would put a large-bore catheter into either the jugular vein of the patient's neck or the large subclavian vein just under the clavicle. It's not a complicated procedure, and ER docs do them all the time, but it's not without risk. I was curious. "Maybe. What's the case?"

"A dehydrated drunk with no good veins."

"I bet you ten dollars that I can start that IV in a vein in his arm on the first try."

Ken and Judy looked at me, and both smiled. I could see they did not believe me. Ken asked, "What makes you think you can do that?"

"It's another trick I learned up in Bryson City that works more times than not."

Ken stuck out his hand to shake. "You're on!"

We walked into the unconscious patient's cubicle. The smell of alcohol was heavy in the air. I took the blood pressure cuff off the wall, applied it to the patient's upper arm, and inflated the cuff. "I'm pumping up the pressure until its 10 to 15 points above his systolic pressure. Then I will hold it there for four to five minutes.

This gives a tourniquet effect, and it is very uncomfortable because the arm becomes anoxic."

"I don't think he'll notice," Judy said.

As each minute went by, the man began to moan from the discomfort. "For patients who are awake, I have to talk them through the temporary pain by explaining that the lack of oxygen relaxes the muscle around the veins, allowing them to dilate and making it easier to start an IV."

I monitored the clock, and at the five-minute mark, I began to let the pressure off the cuff. "I'll let it deflate to about five points above the diastolic," I explained. "This allows the arterial blood to flow into the arm, but it will hold the low-pressure venous blood flow back." I held my breath, but as we watched over the next sixty seconds, the patient's arm began to look like a road map of enlarged and full veins.

"Son of a gun!" Ken exclaimed. "I've never seen anything like that!"

Nodding at Judy, I said, "Want to try now?"

She smiled and quickly inserted a catheter into a dilated arm vein, securing it with tape as I deflated the cuff.

"Well," Ken sighed. "I guess I owe you ten dollars."

Relieved the old trick worked, I countered, "I'll let you buy me a cup of coffee sometime."

Just then, I heard Dolly's voice on the overhead speakers: "Dr. Larimore, stat to L and D. Dr. Walt Larimore, stat to L and D."

"Saw an orderly pushing a pregnant lady in a wheelchair back a few minutes ago. She looked like she was in active labor, and a man followed with two bags slung over his shoulder," Ken commented. "Wonder if they're your patients?"

I jumped up and, once out of the ER, began to sprint.

8

Katie

I RAN THROUGH the double doors leading into the labor and delivery suite.

"Are you Dr. Larimore?" yelled a nurse from the door of one of the two delivery rooms at the far end of the hall.

"Yes!"

"I'm Sandi Lynch. Good to meet you. Now, scrub up quick! One of Dr. Hartman's patients is about to deliver. What size gloves?"

"Eight," I said, running up to the scrub sink, which was just outside the delivery rooms. I grabbed two shoe covers, a head cover, and a mask, and quickly put them on. Looking through the window above the sink into the delivery room as I scrubbed my hands and arms, I could see a tall, young woman in the delivery position. Sandi was cleaning her perineum with Betadine antiseptic solution while another nurse was setting up instruments on a side table. A nursery nurse was preparing the baby bassinet and warmer to receive the little one.

To my surprise, the very top of the baby's head was just visible between the mother's labia, what we call *crowning*, as she cried out in pain during a contraction. A stocky, mustached man with a round face and ruddy cheeks, who I presumed was the father of the baby, was at the woman's side, looking panicked and wearing disposable sterile paper pants, V-neck shirt cover, surgical mask, and head cover. He looked far out of his comfort zone—as do most men in this situation.

I rinsed my arms, backed through the door into the room, dried off, grabbed and quickly put on a sterile gown, and then donned the surgical gloves. The man looked at me with horror and exclaimed, "Just who the heck are *you*? You're *not* Dr. Hartman! We want *our* doctor! *Now!*"

The woman let out another painful moan, pushed, and the baby's head bulged out even more.

"Well, sir, she's about to deliver, and I'm the *only* doctor you have right now! I'm Dr. Hartman's new partner, Dr. Larimore. What are your names?"

He seemed to calm a bit. "I'm Victor Lockwood, and this is my wife, Jennifer. This is our first baby."

"Any problems during pregnancy?" I asked as I began placing the drapes over her legs and abdomen. I could hear the baby's heartbeat on a fetal monitor. The rate and rhythm were normal. I palpated Jennifer's tummy and the baby's head. The position for delivery was perfect.

"No, sir," Victor answered. "Jennifer and the baby have been healthy as can be. No problems until the membranes ruptured at home."

"Prenatal record is clean. No issues at all," said Sandi.

"Vitals?"

"Normal," Sandi said. "Due date is tomorrow."

I smiled. "Tomorrow's my daughter's birthday. But I don't think your little one will wait until then."

Jennifer let out a yelp.

"Okay to push?" Sandi asked.

I nodded, and Sandi had Victor lift Jennifer's head and instructed her to take a deep breath and then give a prolonged push.

As she did, I began to massage the perineum and flex the baby's head. In maternity care, a midwife maxim is that "flexion is your friend." With a vaginal birth, keeping the head flexed presents a smaller circumference, making delivery easier and reducing the likelihood of a tear or the need for a surgical cut called an *episiotomy*. Avoiding either would make recovery both more comfortable and faster for Jennifer.

Jennifer took quick short breaths between contractions. "The next one should do it," I said, trying to sound confident and assured, although my heart was racing. Here I was, a new and untested doctor, at least in this hospital, having to audition in front of new patients, unfamiliar birth attendants, and in a facility using an old-fashioned delivery room and delivery table.

During my medical school days at LSU Charity Hospital in New Orleans and my family medicine residency at Duke, I had been well-trained in these old delivery techniques. But I much preferred the family-friendly birthing suites and midwife techniques we developed in Bryson City—and the professional birth assistants, called *doulas*, who assisted us.[1] If these nurses had not been exposed to this more humane approach, then I expected my plans for after the delivery would be a shock to them.

Jennifer began to moan. Vic lifted her, and Sandi instructed, "Take a deep breath, then give the doctor a long steady push."

As she did, without trauma to the perineal tissues, I delivered the baby's head.

"Jennifer, stop pushing! Pant!" I advised. As she did so, I suctioned the mucus from the baby's nose and mouth. It was clear—neither bloody, which would have suggested trauma, nor meconium-stained, which would have meant the baby passed stool into the amniotic fluid.

Now came the moment that might shock these traditional labor and delivery nurses but create a lifelong memory for this mom and dad. "Victor," I said, "I'd like you to lift Jennifer." She was panting. "Jennifer, I want you to reach down with both your hands and help me deliver your baby." Her eyes widened a bit. She looked at Victor and then me.

"Can I?"

I grinned under my mask as I saw Sandi and the other nurses' eyes enlarge in surprise. Jennifer's contraction began, and she moaned.

"Okay, let's go!"

Victor lifted as Jennifer reached out with both hands. I guided them down to her baby. "Feel the head?" She nodded and smiled. "Okay, give me a push, and let's have a baby." She pushed. I delivered the baby's top shoulder, and then the bottom one, and then I guided Jennifer's hands under her baby's arms and around the trunk.

"Okay, pull your baby up onto your abdomen." She did as instructed. As we guided the little one from her birth canal and onto her belly, I could see the baby was a *she* as the remaining amniotic fluid cascaded into the stainless-steel bucket at my feet. I picked up a sterile blanket and covered the baby. Jennifer and Victor cooed at her and smiled at each other.

"Well come, baby girl Lockwood!" I said. *Well come* was my greeting for every healthy baby I delivered.

There can be so much stress during the birthing process, not only for the family but also for the birth attendants. Seeing and holding a brand-new baby—welcoming them into their life and ours—was an eternally significant event usually accompanied by tears from the baby, the parents, and sometimes even me. It would invariably cause my heart to sing, "It is well, it is well with my soul."[2] The hymn was penned in the 1870s by a man who had just lost four daughters, and it was my wife's favorite, thus my greeting to every newborn: "Well come!" as my soul would worship, "It is well."

"Katie," Jennifer whispered. "*Well* come, little Katherine Jo," she said, mimicking my greeting, as tears streaked down her cheeks.

I grabbed two clamps and attached them to the umbilical cord close to Katie's tummy, leaving about an inch between them. I picked up surgical scissors, blade first, and handed them to Victor. He looked at the instrument and then at me as if to say, *What?* I nodded. "You can cut it."

"Me?" he asked. I didn't dare look at the nurses.

"Of course. It's a way for you to launch her as the newest member of your family."

He took the scissors, and as I gripped the cord, he made a perfect cut. His eyes sparkled, and a smile spread across his face that was obvious even though he wore a mask. I retrieved the scissors and put them back on the edge of the delivery table. Victor, like every other dad who did this, would attest that me letting them sever their child's umbilical cord was one of the most unforgettable parts of the birth for them! In my over fifteen hundred deliveries during my career, I never tired of the elation.

"Are you just going to leave the baby there?" Sandi asked nervously, nodding at the waiting bassinet and warmer.

"I am," I answered, knowing this was against their standard policy and protocol. But it was a birthing method midwives and mothers had used for millennia. However, to assuage the apparent and increasing anxiety of Sandi and the other nurses, I added, "For just a moment more, okay?"

Jennifer's eyebrows furrowed. "I'm feeling a contraction. What do I do?"

I smiled. "It's natural. Your body wants to expel the placenta— the afterbirth. So Victor, why don't you take Katie over to the warmer and help the nurses get her cleaned up and finger- and footprinted. They can even put her hand and footprints on your scrub shirt."

As they did, I felt Jennifer's abdomen. The contraction was beginning. "Give me one last gentle push, Jennifer." As she did, I delivered the placenta into a sterile bowl and examined it. There were no tears or missing pieces that could have remained in the womb and caused bleeding or infection—it was healthy and intact, always a good thing.

"Let me do a quick inspection inside," I told Jennifer. Everything was in order. No tears. No abnormal bleeding. And her uterus was contracting in what would be a several-week journey back to normal size. "Fit as a fiddle," I declared to no one in particular.

The nurses and Victor were busy tending to little Katie, while Jennifer was watching the scene with a satisfied, almost angelic look of rapture and contentment. As a man, I was always mesmerized observing the intense emotions displayed on a woman's face right after birth—expressions revealing her deep feelings of accomplishment, pleasure, appreciation, relief, and happiness, all bubbling out in a divinely designed maternal ecstasy.

A smile spread across her face as tears dropped across her cheeks. *That* smile. I'd seen it several hundred times in medical school, residency, and Bryson City. The bliss of a mother who had just birthed her healthy baby. No more punishing contractions, paroxysms of pain, or arduous pushing. All her hopes and dreams incarnated into her infant. Her sweet expression of achievement and comfort, expectations and possibilities, wrapped into an overflowing emotion of indescribable joy. I never tired of observing this sublime and deeply spiritual moment in the formation of a young family.

I raised the bottom of the table into place and took each of her legs out of its stirrup, massaging each calf as I did so.

"That feels good," she said, as I covered her with a warm blanket and lifted the head of the delivery table.

"We'll get you into a comfortable bed as soon as possible."

She smiled. "That would be nice."

"Just rest and let me go check out Katie."

She nodded. Katie's exam was routine. My first delivery in Kissimmee had gone as well as could have been expected.

Yet one side of me hinted, *You are lucky this went so well.* My compassionate side immediately countered, *No, you are skilled and blessed.* For sure, I was relieved and thrilled.

9

The Journey

WHILE THE NURSES were getting the new family into the recovery room, I went to the doctors' station to dictate a delivery note and write orders for mother and child.

A voice from behind me said, "Got a minute?" It was Sandi. She was quiet a moment. "I'm familiar with midwife techniques, but we don't see them used very often here. We have one female Ob-Gyn who uses some of the newer birthing methods, but most of the male OBs ridicule her for it."

"You don't think I will get in trouble doing things this way?"

She smiled. "Oh, I'm not saying that. I think our other young nurses and our OB nurse supervisor will be supportive. And I, for one, am happy to see it. It's overdue. But some of our older doctors may not be so sympathetic or understanding. I'd recommend you go slow."

"I appreciate the heads-up and support. And the advice."

Sandi turned and left. As I finished my paperwork, several memories flooded my soul. I remembered my junior year of medical school at LSU in New Orleans. They had farmed me out to a branch of Charity Hospital in the small town of Lafayette,

Louisiana, on the border of the Atchafalaya Swamp. After my three classmates and I had finished orientation with the head OB nurse, she asked me to stay behind. Once we were alone, she said, "Your mother called me and told me she's an OB nurse in Baton Rouge."

"When I was younger," I explained, "my mom worked the three to eleven shift, Friday through Sunday, and when she got home, she would wake me to share about the babies she had delivered. For years I thought OB nurses delivered babies, not doctors. She'd tell me stories about the 'good' ones and the 'bad' ones—admiring the skilled physicians and having disdain for the others, which she said were few and far between."

"Your mom told me how very proud she is that one of her boys became a doctor, and I suspect she very much wants him *not* to be a bad one. She told me I was to call her and report if your handwriting is not legible, if you don't clean up after yourself, if you don't treat every patient with the utmost compassion and each and every nurse and staff person with the greatest respect, and if you don't say 'Yes, ma'am,' and 'No, ma'am,' to my staff and me. She told me to ask you, 'Do you understand me?'"

I nodded. "Yes, ma'am."

"One last thing."

There was no telling what was coming next.

"She requested that I put you on call the first night and that I have you sleep on a patient gurney between deliveries."

I must have looked confused because I was. *Why in the world would Mom want that?* I thought.

"She wanted you to know, in some small way, what your patients were experiencing."

After that rotation, I was never the same. The nurses with whom doctors work are invariably competent and compassionate people. They spend far more time with our patients than we doctors do. And I've learned that, in general, female nurses have far more intuition than most male health-care professionals. They can make a doctor's professional life very successful or very uncomfortable.

When I arrived home, Barb and the kids were asleep. I was still revved up from the excitement of my first delivery, so I sat on our swing on the back porch. As I rocked to the calming symphony provided by scores of crickets, katydids, and frogs, I reflected on attending the transition of a baby from unborn to born. It was an exhilarating journey that was an honor to take with a young family—an experience that never exhausted me. Oh, spending hours with a family during labor can tax and tire one, but like our birth patients, we forget the stress, work, and exhaustion it takes to birth a child the instant they release their forceful and hearty first shriek, exclaiming to all, "Look out world! I'm here! I've arrived!"

At birth, the wee one has completed the shortest journey they will ever make. It begins in warmth and darkness, floating in solitude with the comforting lub-dub of their mother's heart. For months they've heard, recognized, and responded to the voice of their parents, especially their mother—they listen to her talking, cooing, singing, reading, and praying. The crossing ends suddenly in bright lights, shrill beeps, and a much colder setting. But once swaddled, warmed, hugged, and welcomed—safe and feeding—the little one can rest and prepare for the greatest expedition of them all—living.

I smiled, remembering little Katie in her bassinet, calmly sucking on her fist. Victor was rapturously studying her, obviously smitten with his tiny little lady. He smiled as her petite fingers grasped his pointer finger, and beamed as he whispered, "Katie."

I walked up beside him. "The same name as my firstborn," I said. Victor grinned.

Katie, like all of us at birth, had never traveled this way before. Fortunately, I thought, we do not have to make this expedition without companions. As the road of life unfolds, we travel side by side—with our parents, clan, friends, teachers, pastors, family doctor, and a loving Creator—as we all share in the marvelous and magnificent voyage from darkness to light.

What always filled me with awe at each birth I attended was that every baby is both the same as every other baby ever born and, at the same time, unique. We are all the same in that we are all created and conceived in the image of God, and because of this, in God's eyes, each of us is both redeemable and worthy of redemption. As his image-bearers, God creates us to glorify himself and fulfill the distinctive role for which he created us while we seek to discover and then enjoy the abundant and full life he designed for those who follow him!

Yet each baby, from conception to physical death, is matchless. No other individual in history will be like them. No other has had or ever will have the same set of fingerprints or brain waves or the same life pathway, perspective, or personality. One of my medical school mentors, a renowned missionary and orthopedic surgeon, Paul Brand, MD, and bestselling author Philip Yancey, cowrote *Fearfully and Wonderfully Made*, which describes the myriad ways each person is knit according to a pattern of incredible purpose. God made us uniquely, in his image, and he made each of us unique.[1]

Katie was.

I loved caring for her throughout her all-too-brief life. She was the first of what Judy named our "End of October Club." All the children we delivered who were born on the last three days of October would come into the office on the same day each year to both celebrate and have their annual well-child checkups. We'd have a party for them with cake or cupcakes, ice cream, and punch. We kept their heights recorded, along with the date and their initials, on the door of one of my exam rooms. Those were joyful days.

Tragically, as a young woman serving our country in the military, Katie contracted a blood cancer that she and her doctors could not defeat. Her family and friends all prayed desperately for a miracle. They *so* wanted her to stay. But her Father in heaven

said, "No, I need her here." She graduated to glory at thirty years of age on April 16, 2016, with her family at her side.

That fall, while researching a book about my father's World War II experiences, I visited Joint Base Myer–Henderson Hall, where Dad had served, and Arlington National Cemetery. I took a few moments to walk over to what is called *Section 55, Site 190*—such a sterile name for Katie's final resting place. "Katherine Jo Lockwood" and "October 29, 1985" had been chiseled into the white marble tombstone. I sat at her feet for a few moments telling her I was glad to have been on call that night, pleased that her dad didn't bounce me out of the delivery room, and delighted to have grown to know, love, and pray for her, her parents, and her two younger brothers.

"As far as I know, you're the first person I delivered who has completed the journey down this remarkable stroll called *life*," I whispered as I gazed across the surrounding verdant grounds covered with similar white markers arranged between and under trees ablaze in their red, yellow, and orange autumnal costumes. I could see her in my mind's eye, strolling toward me, that precious smile of hers shining as it always did. And then she suddenly turned.

Katie! I silently called.

She glanced back.

I'm looking forward to a reunion one day!

She grinned, waved, and skipped away.

I will remember that moment every October 29—as long as my journey continues. And I can't wait to see her again.

10

Our Town

DAN AUTREY AND ONE of our county commissioners, Mike Bast, took Barb and me on an outing to explore an undeveloped piece of property on the shore of Lake Toho as a potential homesite. As we were walking the fields, Mike asked if I knew the origin of the county's name. I guessed they named it after a Seminole Indian called *Chief Osceola*.

Mike laughed. "Lots of folks think that, but it ain't true. His birth name was Billy Powell. His dad was a British trader and his mom a Creek Indian. He was born in Alabama in 1804 and gave himself the name Osceola at a Seminole tribal ceremony around 1820."

"Where were the Seminole Indian native lands?" I asked.

"That's kinda funny," Mike said. "The Seminoles in Florida weren't an actual tribe. They were the loosely organized remnants of other Indian tribes who fled to Florida. When the United States offered to buy Seminole lands to move them to settle on open territory west of the Mississippi, many Seminoles favored the proposal, but not Osceola. He led an uprising opposing the removal. Their guerrilla warfare tactics kept the US military at bay for a long time

in what was called the *Seminole Wars*. The army finally captured Osceola, and he died after only one month in captivity. He was thirty-three years old but never a real chief."

Mike paused for a second, as if deciding whether to go on. "It was reported that an army doctor removed his head as a souvenir and would leave it on the bedposts of children he felt needed discipline."

"I hope you choose *not* to use that form of discipline with Kate and Scott," Dan said.

"Amen!" Barb said.

Movement across the field caught my eye. A flock of wild turkey was emerging from the forest edge.

"Those are Osceola turkeys," said Mike. "Some folks call 'em the Florida turkey. They only live in Central Florida. They're smaller and darker than Eastern Wild Turkey and are named after Osceola. The gobblers can reach three and a half feet tall and weigh up to twenty-five pounds. They make for a great Thanksgiving dinner."[1]

Not appearing the least concerned about the strangers in their midst, the leader of the doting harem was strutting his beautiful plumage. We stood still as the flock walked across the field toward us—rambling closer until several moseyed up to and began pecking on the commissioner's boots.

"Well, I'll be dad-blamed, Commissioner!" Dan exclaimed. "Have you been here feeding these turkeys? Are you baiting 'em up for hunting season?"

Mike's cheeks turned the garnet of a Florida State University athletic uniform, but he did not confess.

Dan and Boots picked us up one Sunday afternoon for a guided tour around town. "Our small-town business district has only one movie theater, the Arcade, and two breakfast joints," Dan said.

"I like Mrs. Mac's," Boots said. "Dan likes Joanie's. So we split our breakfast dates between them."

"Look at the horse!" Scott exclaimed from his car seat.

"That's Makinson's Hardware, the oldest retail hardware store in operation in the state," Boots explained. "It was founded in 1884 by W. B. Makinson, and everyone is drawn to the life-size horse model out front. Been there as long as I can remember!" She pointed. "Barb, here's Shore's Men's Wear right next door to Town and County Women's Boutique. No need to run to Orlando for dress clothes."

"There's a *real* horse!" Scott bellowed.

Sure enough, there was a horse standing outside a store on a side street.

"That's the Saddle Rack," Boots said. "When Dan and I were kids, lots of stores used to have hitching posts out front for folks who rode their horses into town. This is the only one left. It's one of two Western stores in town. The other one, Goold's Department Store, was the first store in Florida to sell Levi jeans."

Barb pointed to the McCrory Dime Store. "Remember, Walt? We had one of those in downtown Baton Rouge when we were growing up."

"It has been here almost fifty years," Dan said. "We have a surprise for you guys, but first I want to show you the redbrick Osceola County Courthouse. It was built in 1890, and it is the oldest courthouse in active use in Florida."

It was an imposing structure. Its architectural elements included a cupola above the entrance, round arches on the portico and above the doors, and segmental arches above all the windows.

Dan pulled into a lakeside park. "You have to see our most unique and auspicious tourist attraction."

Boots moaned. "Dan, can't we skip this atrocity?"

"They need to see the good, the bad, and the ugly," he replied, laughing.

"It qualifies for the last two characteristics," Boots said.

"The Monument of the States!" Dan exclaimed, pointing toward a fifty-foot-tall monolithic conglomeration of various-sized squares and rectangles, each containing words and objects.

"It's hideous," Barb whispered.

"Walt, it was conceived by a retired physician after the Japanese attack on Pearl Harbor as a symbol of America. It was built by volunteers, using donated stones and artifacts sent by the governors of forty-three states, as well as everyday citizens from every state and twenty-one countries. It is made of more than fifteen hundred stones and includes meteors, stalagmites, petrified wood, teeth and bones, and even a rock from President Franklin D. Roosevelt's estate in New York. It's called *The Most Unique Tourist Attraction in the World*."

"Well, it's certainly unique!" was all I could think to say.

"Look," Barb said, pointing, "near the top. It says, 'Harvard Medical School.'"

"I graduated from Harvard," I told Dan. He looked surprised.

"I thought you went to LSU."

"Well, we call LSU *Harvard on the Bayou*."

As we drove north of the city limits, Barb leaned over to me and whispered, "This town is darling."

Boots pointed out the headquarters of the Tupperware Corporation.

"A man by the name of Earl Silas Tupper founded it," Dan said.

"Thus, the term *Tupperware*," Boots added. "It's now world-famous for home parties where they sell their air-tight plastic containers used for food storage."

"I have a bunch of them," Barb said. Her voice deepened as she imitated a popular advertisement: "With their patented burping seal, which distinguishes them from their competitors."

"You've been watching far too much TV," Boots said, laughing.

"Right up here," Dan added, "we have another of Kissimmee's world-famous attractions, Gatorland. Boots and I would like to take you all, if that's okay."

The kids cheered as we pulled up and parked. We walked through a giant replica of a gator's mouth widely open. As Dan bought tickets, Barb pointed to a sign that read, "The Alligator Capital of the World." A high school student gave us a brief tour.

"Gatorland houses countless alligators and crocodiles of all sizes, from babies, known as *grunts*, to fourteen-foot monsters. Don't miss our two-thousand-feet-long swamp walk over our breeding marsh. The producers of the movie *Indiana Jones and the Temple of Doom*, filmed just last year, used our breeding marsh as a set for parts of the movie. We have tall observation towers there so you can be on the lookout for our rare albino, or leucistic, alligators."

The kids laughed in glee during a show called the *Gator Jumparoo* in which some of their jumping alligators would lunge out of the water to snag pieces of chicken held four to five feet above the water. I enjoyed the Alligator Wrestling Show; however, Dan, Boots, Scott, and Kate most enjoyed the ride around and through the attraction on a small steam-driven train. As we left the park, Scott, but *not* Kate, had pictures taken with a baby alligator (with a band holding its powerful jaws shut) and a boa constrictor!

"This is old Florida at its best!" Dan exclaimed as we drove away. I had no reason to argue. Our admiration and affection for the Autreys were growing daily. I secretly wondered if they might not become honorary parents for us and grandparents for our kids.[2]

11

Commencement

By the end of my first month practicing with John, I was beginning to fall into a rhythm. I would make rounds at the hospital early in the morning and then drive to the office to enjoy a cup of coffee while reviewing the charts of my morning patients. Judy Simpson, who had just started working at our office, walked up and added a few charts to my in-box.

"Good morning," I said.

"Morning, Walt. Hey, Dan Autrey is here to see you. Says he only needs a second. He doesn't look well."

"Bring him back."

My internal alarm spiked when Dan walked in. His countenance was drooped, his face despondent, and when he saw me, his eyes brimmed with tears. He was shaking, looked devastated, and as his head dropped, he began to weep. I stood up and put my arm around his shoulders as they heaved.

"Dan, what's the matter?"

He sniffled, sighed, and tried to stand erect as he looked across my office and out the window overlooking a small lake. He whispered, "She's gone."

"Who?"

He turned back to me. "Boots! I woke up and rolled over to kiss her as I do every morning. She was cold and didn't move. I called 9-1-1, and they were there in minutes. There was nothing they could do."

"Here, sit." I guided him to a sofa.

"She's suffered for years from debilitating migraines and had some congestive heart failure; however, as you well know, she never let it show or slow her down. Although most people, even herself given the pace she kept, thought she was in excellent health, I knew with her CHF she wasn't. But she had no recent complaints, just her usual bubbly self. Last night her daughter Debby came over for a visit. They had a great time. Then we attended a party with old friends at the Silver Spurs Club. Being an introvert, I don't enjoy social events very much, but Boots does. She flits from person to person, making them comfortable, laughing with them, and then moving to the next. Our pastor likens her to a hummingbird because of her beauty, constant movement, excitement, and definition of purpose. Boots was always a joy."

He took a deep breath, and I grabbed a box of tissues. He pulled a couple to wipe his eyes and blow his nose. "The medical examiner insists on an autopsy. I don't want one." He lowered his head.

"Given it was an unattended death, Dan, by law, he must. What he finds may be helpful to the kids and grandkids."

He sniffled and nodded. "I came by to get medication for my nerves and to help me sleep in case I need them."

"Of course," I said. I pulled a prescription pad out of my white coat and began to write. "I'm writing three prescriptions. One will calm your nerves. The second will help you sleep. And there's a third one I'd like to give you. I want to prescribe a few verses for you to read, meditate on, pray over, and maybe even memorize."

He raised his eyebrows but nodded.

I wrote John 11:35 and explained, "This verse tells how Jesus wept at the grave of his good friend, Lazarus."

Dan stopped me. "I've never understood that, Walt. Jesus knew Lazarus was dead before being told. He knew he would raise him from the dead. So why'd he weep?"

"That's a great question, Dan. The only reason I've ever come up with is that he knows the world is full of pain and suffering, regret and loss, and depression and devastation. I'm guessing he wept because knowing the end of a great story doesn't mean we won't cry at the sad parts."

Dan nodded.

I scribbled Matthew 5:4. "Maybe that's why Jesus told us, 'Blessed are those who mourn, for they will be comforted.' Dan, it's painful to mourn and grieve, but it's healthy to let it out. I don't believe we can heal from the tremendous shock of death without it. And if we look for God in the storm, he *will* provide his peace."

He nodded again as tears spilled down his face.

"Dan, for Christians, death isn't the end. It's a passageway, a commencement, from an often troubled and painful life on earth to eternal life in heaven with Christ. In an instant, we graduate to glory. You'll see her again, Dan." I sensed a lump rising in my throat and my lips quivering. "And so will I."

"But it's still hard. I just don't know what the future will hold for me without her."

"Barb and I are learning we can entrust the future we cannot see to the God who can."

Dan smiled and said, "One of my children said I don't have to know what's in my future if I know *who* holds it in his hands."

I jotted down several other Bible verses. "That's why I'm giving you this third prescription."

He took it. "I appreciate them all."

I sensed a leading: *It wouldn't hurt to offer a prayer.* But my other side said, *He came for medicine, not a sermon. You've definitely preached way too much. You should do your job, and let the pastor do his! Don't want him to think you're a Jesus freak, do you?*

My calmer side argued, *But it's never wrong to pray. Doesn't the Bible say, "Rejoice always, pray continually, give thanks in all circumstances; for this is God's will for you"?*[1]

"Dan, I believe that if you can draw closer to God during this difficult time, he himself will comfort you and hold you close." I paused, feeling nervous. After a deep breath and with trepidation, I asked, "May I pray with you?"

He nodded his permission, and I shared a short prayer. I thanked the Lord for the blessing Boots had been in the lives of Dan, their children, my family, and our community. I asked for peace and comfort for him and his family. We said, "Amen," and he hugged me. Praying with Dan was not only less nerve-racking than I thought it would be, but it was also empowering to me and encouraging to him.

He folded the prescriptions, put them in his shirt pocket, and blew his nose. "You'll never know what this means, Walt," he whispered. "Thanks."

"God's Word and prayer, along with friends and family, have been an incredible comfort and anchor for me during various trials in my life. This was true when Barb and I grieved through the shock of learning that Kate had cerebral palsy and when we lost a child to miscarriage. It was even more critical when we suffered through the horrible circumstances that led us away from Bryson City. Barb and I are learning firsthand the encouragement and peace Scripture and prayer can give us in times of trouble."

Dan nodded.

I smiled. "I must admit, I was nervous about offering to pray with you."

He took both of my hands in his. "Don't be. Don't ever be. He's the Great Physician. Bring him to your patients and your patients to him."

That interaction was a turning point for me. In medical school and residency, I had heard it said that religion and spirituality had no place in medicine—certainly no place in patient encounters.

But in Bryson City, I had prayed with some patients, as anxiety-provoking as that was. Now I heard a voice whispering to my heart, *Maybe it's time to put God's Word and prayer into your spiritual black bag. They will be two of the most powerful tools you'll have as a family physician.* I shushed my mind before my nefarious side could reply.

"Thanks, Dan," I said. "That's a real encouragement for me. I appreciate it."

"No," he replied. "Thank you for everything." He nodded and added, "She sure loved you, Barb, and your kids."

"I'll be with you every step of the way, Dan. I'm here whenever you need me. More importantly, God is with you, my friend."

He nodded, smiled, and as he walked down the hall, Judy approached my office. "Your first patient is waiting. But do you need a moment?"

"I think I'm okay. Let's hit it."

She smiled. "What you did for him was special; care and caring—the best medicine *and* a powerful combination."

"It's an honor," I whispered.

12

Forgiveness

My mind flashed back to a time Dan and Boots had once showered me with undeserved forgiveness after a misdiagnosis. Dan had come to the office after developing a sharp midback pain while using a shovel. He wasn't too uncomfortable but had muscle spasms. I diagnosed a muscle strain and prescribed an anti-inflammatory and a muscle relaxant.

Boots dragged him to my office the next morning and pointed a finger at me saying, "It's *not* a pulled muscle. It's something else. Because of the pain, he wasn't able to lie flat and spent the night in his recliner. Worst yet, he kept *me* awake. So you need to find out what is causing this and fix it *now*—for his, my, and *your* sake."

I had Judy take an X-ray that revealed the source of Dan's pain—an osteoporotic compression fracture of his twelfth thoracic vertebra—what we call *T12*. He had a family history of thin bones, osteoporosis, but I had never tested him for it. I felt overwhelming guilt.

You're an embarrassment, my malevolent side said. *Why didn't you consider it? Look how old and frail he is.* My better side tried to console me: *But an atraumatic compression fracture is far less common than a muscle strain. And he had a muscle spasm.*

The base side hissed, *Now you could be in big trouble. Pillars of the community like this can spread the news of your mistake far and wide. Don't you dare tell them!* My superior voice countered, *For now, you let them know what happened and then give them the excellent care they'll need during what will be a very painful and very long convalescence.*

I explained to Dan and Boots the diagnosis and what we needed to do now, beginning with a lightweight brace for him to wear around his trunk, from his hips to under his arms, to prevent unnecessary pain or more damage from excessive movement. We discussed using ice, heat, and oral nonsteroidal anti-inflammatories, such as ibuprofen, alternated every two hours with acetaminophen. I prescribed an oral narcotic to take for severe pain and cautioned them concerning possible mental and gastrointestinal side effects along with the small but real risk of addiction if taken for too long.

"Are there any other options?" Boots said.

"There's always the hospital for IV medications, but before that, I'd recommend another choice that's not too expensive and is safer." I explained that a hormone made by the thyroid gland, calcitonin, helps strengthen bones and reduce pain in people with acute compression fractures from osteoporosis. I explained, "Salmon calcitonin is the best choice because it's less expensive, more potent, and longer lasting than human calcitonin. Also, it's available in an easy-to-use daily injection. Boots, I can get Judy to show you how to do it at home."

"Are there any downsides?" Boots asked.

"So far, it's approved by the FDA only to treat osteoporosis and not for acute compression fractures from osteoporosis. But European studies show it works for these types of fractures, so I can prescribe it as what's called *off-label use.* It's worked well with some other patients."

Boots said, "Where do we sign?"

They started the therapy, and I was delighted to learn Dan's pain subsided in hours—a relief for all three of us. Within six weeks, his back X-ray was showing healing. I ordered a baseline bone density scan and began treatment for Dan's osteoporosis, aiming to prevent a hip fracture or another vertebral fracture.

Later, Dan and I talked of my misdiagnosis and how surprised I was he had not gotten angry and looked for another doctor.

Dan told me, "The fact that you admitted what had happened, apologized for it, and did everything in your power to make it better increased our already high level of trust and confidence in you, Doc."

Taking a deep breath and releasing a sigh of relief, I sensed my merciless angel would say something about my being lucky once again.

"I've learned that when someone does something that injures or hurts me," Dan said, "I can never heal until I forgive them. It turns out *not* forgiving is harmful to my mental *and* physical health." Dan smiled and patted me on the back. "Besides, Doc, the Good Book teaches that Christians are to be 'kind and compassionate to one another, forgiving each other, just as in Christ God forgave' us. That's in the book of Ephesians."[1]

"I appreciate your friendship and your forgiveness, Dan," I stammered. "But I'm not sure I deserve it. That mistake and the pain it caused you still haunt me."

"Doc, you're forgiven."

"I'm thankful for that, but I'm not sure I'd be as gracious if it were me."

Dan thought a moment. "Our pastor taught us that those who have received God's mercy but refuse to share it with others can become imprisoned by bitterness or revenge. But when we encounter God's grace and share it with others, the prisoner we set free is ourselves. Unjust and spiteful actions by hateful people have hurt me in the past. So forgiving, to me, doesn't mean not enforcing consequences or boundaries; it doesn't mean forgetting, because I can't do that. But it means giving up vindictiveness or bitterness—releasing my right to hurt someone else for hurting me. I'm learning to leave the final reckoning to the Lord."

"That's good, Dan. I like that. Thanks."

"Doc, it's easy for me to forgive when I realize that the Lord has forgiven me for much, much worse." He chuckled, leaned over, and whispered, "But what's far better is that Boots has forgiven you. That's worth its weight in gold in this town. And that's a fact!"

13

Funeral

THE LARGEST CHURCH in town, First United Methodist Church, hosted Boots's funeral rather than the Autreys' home church, Pleasant Hill Presbyterian Church. They expected a large attendance because of Boots's pioneer family and her community activities. It was no surprise to those who knew and loved Jeannette Overstreet "Boots" Autrey that the service was standing room only.

Boots was a fourth-generation member of the Overstreets, one of Osceola County's pioneer ranching families. Her great-grandfather, Henry Overstreet, had moved from Georgia to what is now Osceola County in 1852. Historical documents record that the Overstreet clan was driving a herd of cattle to Tampa when they stopped at Osceola County's Bonnet Creek because of rising floodwaters. Never leaving, they joined the other pioneer families who carved out a living and homesteads from among the oak hammocks and palm tree groves, draining and filling thick cypress swamps, while developing cattle ranches and orange groves. They were rural, pedestrian folk who loved God, one another, their churches, their community, the land, their livestock, and their country.

Growing up on her family's large cattle ranch, Boots was never much of a cowgirl; however, her family said that as a child she often climbed into her daddy's boots, and the nickname *Boots* stuck. Everybody loved Boots. She gave her heart, her time, and her money to multiple local charities and civic events, serving as First Lady of Osceola County and Florida's Outstanding Cattlewoman. No wonder that when John, Cleta, Barb, and I arrived late, we were fortunate to find seats in the balcony.

The outpouring of love, admiration, and humorous recollections was heartwarming. The pastor described Boots as his favorite hummingbird, saying she had the spiritual gift of *flitting*—of spreading the pollen of grace, mercy, friendship, and love to each person she visited. That analogy made me smile.

At the reception, while Dan, his sister Connie, and the children greeted friends, I noticed Geech sitting with a distinguished-looking, elderly gentleman. He was short with white hair, bushy white eyebrows, and ruddy cheeks. Geech waved me over.

"Doc, how 'bout taking a seat and joining us a spell?"

"I'd be happy to."

"I want to introduce you to my friend Russell Thacker."

As we shook hands and I sat, Geech said, "Russell is a native and a county institution—served at various times on the Kissimmee City Commission and even as the mayor of Kissimmee. He's an attorney who worked for years as an Osceola County judge. He and his wife, Edna, have been married over forty years, and they have six adult children, all of whom live here. They met in Beaumont, Texas, where they lived in the same boardinghouse. She had finished nurse's training and had her first job as an RN. He was working in the shipyard waiting to go into the navy."

"Probably more than you ever wanted to know," the man scowled.

"Good to meet you, Judge Thacker," I said.

"Just call me Russell."

I nodded and turned to Geech. "I'm sorry for your loss."

He adjusted his Stetson. "It's gonna be a lot harder for Dan and Connie, I'll tell ya that."

Russell said, "Geech, I saw the *Orlando Sentinel* article about you and your clan. You see it?"

"Nope. I heard about it, but I don't read the paper very much."

The judge smiled. "They said you and your brothers are the kind of men Frederic Remington depicted in his paintings and sculpture, and that y'all were the spitting images of the cowboys Louis L'Amour has written about for years. They called y'all 'quintessential cowboys' and said the Partin clan are 'Kissimmee's answer to the Ewings of Dallas'—that y'all were all born and bred on the range and that doubtlessly you all will die there too—with your boots on, of course."

"Sounds to me like only that last sentence is an accurate one, Russell," Geech said.

"When we were kids," Russell said, "my brother, Clarence, and I would go over to the Partins' big ole two-story ranch house over on Fish Lake, between Kissimmee and St. Cloud. Geech, I remember y'all had your own electricity generator."

Geech nodded. "My daddy, Henry O. Partin, built that house in the early '30s. It was one of the first houses in rural Osceola County to have electricity back when electric power was only in town."

"Tell Doc about y'all's phone system."

Geech laughed. "Later, after we boys had our own houses on the ranch, Daddy put in his own private phone system that connected all our households so he could call us each morning and direct us where to assemble for work that day. It was just a humble little ole family ranch."

"Don't believe him, Doc. There was a *Saturday Evening Post* reporter who came out here in the '50s to do a feature story on the Partins. Called 'em 'the hardest working millionaires in America.'"

Geech sneered. "What that fool couldn't understand is that the average rancher is land and stock rich but cash poor. In fact, our entire extended Partin family had only a single checking account. Every son could sign checks, but the balance was carefully tallied by Daddy and Mama. They knew where every dime went—what few there were."

"The reporter wrote that your pop had built his empire without hiring a single cowboy."

"He didn't have to!" Geech said, snickering. "He and Mama raised all the cowboys they needed."

"Well, you and your siblings are doing your part, aren't 'cha?"

Geech smiled. "Collectively, we're at fifteen children and fifty grandchildren."

"Doc, Geech won't tell you, but their *Heart Bar Ranch* is known far and wide for breeding Brahman cattle that they imported from India."

"Well, we didn't import 'em," Geech said. "It was in 1933 that Daddy took me and my brother Slim to Alice, Texas. Daddy purchased 150 head 'cause we heard from the Texan ranchers that Brahmans were better suited to hot, humid weather than most breeds. I tell ya, it was a big day in Kissimmee when the cattle train arrived."

"That's not all you came back with, is it, Geech?" Russell said, looking mischievous.

"Judge, you didn't have to bring that up, did you?"

"Doc," Russell explained, "Geech brought back a Quarter Horse, a breed that got its name from the fact that they are extremely fast at running the quarter mile."

"That's where I laid my eyes on a Quarter Horse for the first time," said Geech. "I saw how agile they were at herding cattle. The Texan ranchers said they were known for their cow sense. Daddy, Slim, and I watched 'em outmaneuver the cattle every time, and I was particularly impressed with their calm disposition. I thought they'd be ideal horses for our ranch. Daddy agreed and let me purchase what would be the first registered Quarter Horse in Florida."

Russell's smile spread ear to ear. "I remember when that pony arrived. Remember it like it was yesterday. Tell Doc about it, Geech!"

"I didn't want its arrival to go unnoticed. After all, I paid $150, a small fortune at the time, for that blue-blooded new mount. So I made sure there was an audience at the train station in Kissimmee when they unloaded my Quarter Horse. I was as proud as a peacock. There were folks from the newspaper, politicians, and other ranchers—and, obviously, a local lawyer or two." He bent his head toward Russell just to be sure I knew to whom he was referring. "But what I had planned as a moment of personal triumph for me, my family, and our ranch was one of the biggest embarrassments of my life." He chuckled, coughed, and sipped some juice.

"What happened?" I asked.

"Turns out my Quarter Horse was shipped in one of the cattle cars, and them Brahman rascals had completely chewed off his mane and tail." Geech chuckled and slapped his knee. "When he came out of that boxcar, he was the most pitiful creature I'd ever seen—more meant to be shot than saluted. I was the laughingstock around town for a while. But I'll tell ya what, I got the last laugh. My horse's hair grew back, and his unwanted haircut did nothing to diminish his speed."

Russel interjected, "And y'all ran him for an occasional race for money. Ain't that true, Geech?"

I think Geech blushed.

"Well, what we knew that no one else around these parts knew was that racing a normal cow pony against a Quarter Horse over a quarter-mile course is like racing a Chevy Nova against a Ferrari." He laughed. "And when you own the first Quarter Horse in the state, racing is a particularly rewarding experience. I'd work cattle with that horse five days a week, and then Slim, who only weighed about 135 or 140 pounds at the time, would ride him in races on Saturdays and Sundays. I remember a feller saying my horse didn't look to be as fast as a fat washwoman, and he put up a whole fistful of money against us. Daddy matched every dime. Well, I'll tell you what. My little pony took the race going away."

"And you took the money going away, didn't ya?" Russell said.

"For quite a few years," Geech added, laughing. "Doc, you and your boy come out some weekend, and we'll ride a bit. It'll be good for you both. The old cowboys always say, 'There is something about the outside of a horse that is good for the inside of a man.'"[1]

14

Hummingbird

A FEW WEEKS after Boots's death, Dan showed up at the practice and waited in my office while I finished with my last patient.

"I just wanted to come by," he began, "and thank you for being there for me during a difficult time."

I gestured to the sofa, and he had a seat. "It was my honor, Dan. How are you doing?"

"After the funeral, I was despondent. I began thinking the reason God took Boots was that I loved her more than him. I don't know, but I couldn't shake the sadness and gloom I was feeling. I didn't doubt my faith and still felt close to God. But part of me was *so* lost." He sighed as his eyes watered. "I always had so much peace up in the mountains, so I went to Bryson City, to open up our second home, let it air out a bit, and just spend some time with nature and the Lord."

"I remember some wonderful meals and visits we had during our four years there," I said. "And I'll always remember Boots constantly pitching us to move down here."

Dan laughed. "Well, it worked, didn't it?"

"And I'm grateful."

"I rode up with a couple from Kissimmee who own the cabin next door—Chuck and Dee Parsons. Have you met Chuck?"

I shook my head.

"He's an architect who opened his office in Kissimmee about twenty-five years ago. He was the city's only architect. Two of his boys, Dale and Ray, have followed in his footsteps as architects. Anyway, after the ten-hour drive up there, we went to Ingles Market to stock up on groceries and made it up to our cabins on the ridge above the Nantahala River by late afternoon. I unloaded my luggage and supplies. The Parsonses wanted to share dinner, but I told them I needed to be alone. I opened up the house and put out the bird feeders. You'll remember how many migrating birds we get up there."

"I loved seeing them every spring."

"Boots and I both had a great love and fascination for the little beauties, especially the hummingbirds, and did all we could to attract them. So I set out three feeders. I wanted them to have food for the next morning. I wanted to enjoy their company. I checked the mailbox, and to my surprise, I had a card from Scotland from my granddaughter, Abbie, with a beautiful hummingbird embossed on the front. She wrote that it reminded her of her Grandboo. This did not prepare me for what was to follow, but it did later help me understand what happened."

"Color me curious," I said.

"Well, before I knew it, a small army of ruby-throated hummingbirds was at the feeders, arguing and fighting with each other. It was the most hummers I had ever seen. Soon, the air surrounding the cabin was full of their gyrations, and I thought about Boots missing the greatest show we had ever had in the twenty-six years we enjoyed the cabin."

He took a deep breath, smiled, and let it out. "Oh, how I like to watch them, especially when they're aggravated, which it seems to me is their nature. Their aerial skirmishes can continue for long stretches of time. They're not afraid of anything that might come along. I have seen one of those hummers chase a crow and another attack a hawk that had the nerve to fly into his territory."

His face became serious. "A neighbor, Herb, whose cabin is just below ours, stepped up on my deck for a visit. I glanced at my watch. It was 7:00 p.m. and a cool, sixty-degree, windy evening. Then the strangest thing happened. We had been standing there for only a minute when we both looked down, and there lay a beautiful little female hummingbird at my feet."

"What happened?"

"Birds would sometimes fly into our sliding-glass doors. I think the reflection of the trees confused them. What was unusual was that I didn't hear a thump when she struck it, as I usually do when this happens—probably because she was so small. I hoped she was only stunned, so I gently picked her up and cupped her in my hands so that the warmth might help revive her—peeking in from time to time to see if she was recovering. In a short while, when I looked in, she was peeking out. I attempted to set her down out of the wind, so she could fly away when able. Herb and I were both stunned when she flitted up to perch on my right shoulder."

"Had something like that ever happened before?"

"I've studied and watched hummingbirds for decades, but I never knew of one doing this. Oh, Boots and I could get them to land on our fingers next to the feeder but never land on *us*. And that bird stayed and stayed and wouldn't leave. After about five minutes, my neighbor said he needed to get dinner started, and there I stood, turning to protect my little friend from the cold and wondering why I hadn't asked Herb to get a picture of all this. Each time I cocked my head around and glanced down at her, she turned her head around and stared at me. I wanted to go inside the cabin for a camera but knew if she flew off inside, it would be difficult to get her out without harming her."

His eyes misted. "Doc, I began to wonder a crazy thought. I said, 'Boots, is that you?' Well, you know what she did? She flew off my shoulder to about a foot in front of my face. I couldn't believe my eyes, but I'd swear she nodded her little head. Then she flew back on my shoulder." He paused and looked into my eyes. "Do you think I'm nuts?"

"I don't, my friend," I replied. But I *was* wondering what was real and what was imagined.

"I began to talk to her. I laughed, remembering all the years working with friends at the Silver Spurs and volunteering for so many community and church activities. Then I talked about our years taking the Boat-a-Cade trips right here from Lake Toho to the Keys or the east or west coast of Florida. And I talked about growing older without her."

He took a deep breath. "Then I told her how sad I was that she left me. Left me alone—unprepared to go on without her." He looked up, tears falling down his cheeks. "I told her I didn't know what I would do without her, how I would get along. Not sure I even wanted to. But I figured I would . . . somehow." He took out a handkerchief and blew his nose. "Then it was as if I could hear her voice—actually hear her voice: 'Dan Autrey, you listen to me.' I could just see her wagging her pointer finger at me like she did the day she fussed at you."

I smiled.

"She said, 'You've got the Lord, you've got the Word of God, you've got our kids and grandkids, you've got the folks at church, and you've got a great community. You pick yourself up, and you get on with life. Do you hear me? And if you will not do it for yourself and them, then you do it for me.'"

He chuckled. "Some of the best counsel I've ever received. And it didn't cost a dime."

I laughed with him.

"Well, it was getting dark. All the other birds had left. So I stood up and told her she could go. I even tried to shake her off gently. She wouldn't leave."

"What did you do?"

"Since Chuck and Dee were at their house, next door, I decided to go there for a picture. I walked sideways to protect her from the cold wind; she was hanging on for dear life. We were constantly checking on each other and made it to the Parsonses' deck. They were watching TV, but when they looked up and saw us standing outside their picture window, Chuck hollered, 'I'll be darned!' and they dashed out and gawked at us. Their eyes were as wide as saucers. Dee said, 'Dan, there's a hummingbird on your shoulder.' I looked at the little bird, and she looked at me.

"Chuck said, 'Let me grab a camera.' They took several pictures of me alone and of me with each of them. I thanked them for telling me I wasn't crazy, said goodnight, and hurried to my back patio."

"She was still on your shoulder?"

"She was, but it was dark. I knew she needed to go to her nest for warmth and rest. So I told her that I would be fine, and I would never forget her; I would never be the same, but I would learn to get along without her, and I would heal. I thanked her for loving me—for loving me well. I asked her to get our home in heaven ready, to tell all our friends, family, and loved ones who had passed before hello for me and that I would join her up there one day. Then I said goodbye."

Dan lowered his head for a moment. It was a sacred silence. He looked up and confided, "Do you know what happened?"

I shook my head. "I have *no* clue."

"She didn't move. I turned my head and looked at her and said, 'Honey, we're both getting too cold. Why don't you go find a nice warm place?' She tilted her head, stared up at me, and whoosh!— flew so fast I didn't see her leave. Then there she was hovering a foot or so in front of my face. Then she zoomed away. I laughed. I did. I glanced at my watch, and it was 7:35. I was so grateful to the Lord for sending my Boots back as a hummingbird angel. That's what I believe happened. I do."

Maybe he saw a glance of skepticism or doubt—perhaps astonishment. Physicians hear many wonderful, horrific, and strange stories from their patients. Some are believable; some are not. It comes with the territory. Healthy skepticism is wise—like the Berean Christians whom Paul the apostle complimented for receiving what he said but only after checking the evidence to be sure "what Paul said was true."[1]

Dan smiled and shook his head ever so slightly as if recognizing my suspicion. He reached into his shirt pocket and pulled out some pictures. "The next day about noon, the Parsonses knocked on my door. When I opened it, they thrust these into my hands."

He handed several pictures to me.

"They had taken the film into town for the one-hour development at Super Swain Drug Store."

I sorted through them. They were nice. Dan by himself; Dan with Dee; Dan and Chuck.

"Look closely," he said softly.

I did. I felt my eyes widen in amazement as my jaw dropped. "There's no hummingbird! Not in one picture, Dan," I mumbled, continuing to flip through them.

"Not one!" he said, grinning from ear to ear, his face beaming. Dan sniffled and was quiet a moment.

"Wow!" was all I could say.

"Hummingbirds will always be with me."

"I can certainly see why."

"When I got home yesterday, there was a package in the mail addressed to Boots from a greeting card company. On the outside, it said, 'A Gift to You.' Inside was a box of beautiful hummingbird cards. I believe this was God's way of showing me that Boots will always be with me."

Dan laughed. "An angel for sure!" he exclaimed, his face beaming. As he laughed, tears of joy rolled down his cheeks.[2]

PART THREE

15

A New Home

AFTER BEING IN OUR RENTAL HOME for six months, it was a treat to move into the ranch-style home we purchased on Starfish Street less than three miles from the hospital and my office.

"A perfect name for a Florida street," Barb commented.

"If we lived at the seashore," I retorted. "The nearest beach is over fifty miles away."

"I think it's a charming name for a street. It's one block from Dolphin Street, and aren't porpoises your favorite marine animal? Wasn't your nickname Flipper when you were a kid because you were such a great swimmer?"

"I'm certain that dolphins inhabit Lake Toho, and starfish litter the shores," I quipped.

"You're incorrigible!" Barb said. "I think the street names are adorable."

When Kevin Cole had shown us the home, he commented, "The open great room has a high-vaulted ceiling next to a sunken sitting area and a large wood-burning fireplace. The kitchen has plenty of workspaces, top-notch cabinetry, and a closet pantry, which are all pluses. But perhaps the big draw is the massive covered and screened back porch." He added, "It's the pride of the home, with exposed beams, a fireplace-grill combo, and a huge hot tub—big enough for the entire family." He was right. In fact, Kate and Scott both learned to swim in that hot tub! We also loved that it overlooked a private yard with large oak trees along the back property line. The front yard boasted a large maple tree.

"Look at this," Kevin said, walking us from the back porch through French doors into the master bedroom. "The master suite has a roomy walk-in closet, dual vanities, and a most unique shower." He pulled the shower curtain, and the entire back wall was a sliding glass door that opened to a small, completely enclosed private sitting porch. "You don't see *that* every day. Also, the majestic oak trees shade the house and keep the afternoon temperatures ten to fifteen degrees cooler."

We were enamored with it almost immediately.

"You'd be only the sixth owners of this property, purchased by a fellow named Hamilton Disston, who bought four million acres of Central Florida from the US government in 1881, bailing the state out of its debt and becoming the largest single landowner in the United States. A local ranching family, then a developer, then the people who built the house in 1978 all followed. And now you. How many people have a property deed like that?"

Kevin shared the neighborhood's history as he walked us around, introducing us to the neighbors. "This very property served as the location of the first arena for the Silver Spurs Riding Club. It was part of Geech and Connie Partins' ranch. You've met them, right?"

I nodded.

"They staged a Western show right here in March 1944 as their contribution to the war efforts. The admission to the event was the purchase of a war bond, and about one thousand people—about a third of the local population—attended.

"That success led them to add some stalls and a grandstand for their first full-dress rodeo on July 4, 1944. That too was a rousing success, so they held them here every summer until 1949 when the club purchased fifteen acres out on US 192, the major highway between Kissimmee and St. Cloud, and built the Silver Spurs Rodeo Arena that's still there. It seats over eight thousand folks and also hosts Osceola Kowboy football games. Later they added the fairgrounds and started holding the rodeo twice a year. They pair their large rodeo in February with the annual Kissimmee Valley Livestock Show and Osceola County Fair. You can't miss those events. Everyone in the county attends. They're great fun."

An elegant woman stepped out of the corner house across the street and waved. "Hello, Kevin!" She was short and thin, crowned with thick white hair cropped short. Her smile was welcoming, and her blue eyes sparkled as she walked toward us.

"This will be a treat," Kevin said to us. "Hello, Edna! Let me introduce you to your new neighbors." As we shook hands, he added, "Edna's husband, Russell, is a retired judge and well known in these parts for his public service."

Edna laughed. "Don't listen to Kevin. My husband is best known for marrying me—his wonderful wife!"

"I met him at Boots's funeral."

"He mentioned that, Dr. Larimore."

"Walt's fine."

I detected a Cajun accent. "Are you by any chance from Louisiana?"

"Mais, oui!" Edna answered. "But how could you tell? It wouldn't be my brogue?" she asked, laughing.

"We were both raised in Baton Rouge!" Barb exclaimed.

"Well, ma cher," Edna said, "it will be good to have more Louisiana people in the neighborhood!"

After walking the neighborhood, Barb asked about the dirt road behind the stately oak trees that bordered our backyard.

"It's called *Aultman Road*. I want to show you something at the end of the road. It's only a short way."

As we walked down the road, I noticed some movement—something was slowly dropping from a tree branch that was six feet off the ground. I instantly knew what it was: an exceptionally large, yellow and red, six- to seven-foot snake. I sprinted toward the tree, leaped across the ditch, bounding back to my childhood, and quickly grabbed the serpent behind its head as it tried valiantly to escape.

Its smooth, silky scales were a striking yellow-to-orange hue. I was thrilled to capture such a beautiful creature, and I proudly showed it to Kevin, Barb, and the kids. "It's called a corn snake or a red rat snake," I boasted. "They vary in color from yellowish to orange with large red blotches on their backs." As I held it out, Scott rubbed his hand on the glistening smooth scales. Barb and Kate definitely *did not*! I added, "Isn't it beautiful?" The males nodded; the females vehemently shook their heads and grimaced.

"What are you going to do with *that*?" Barb asked.

"Let's keep him, Dad!" Scott exclaimed.

Barb's eyes instantly vetoed that idea.

"How about we take him down and let him go on the property I'm going to show you?" Kevin asked.

We came to a small bridge crossing a canal from which we could see a Spanish-style, tiled-roof mansion on the shore of Lake Toho. "That's the old Tupper Mansion. Earl Tupper, the founder of Tupperware, purchased it in 1952, along with its nineteen hundred feet of lake frontage. The home had one of the few indoor swimming pools in the county. A natural spring filled the pool, and the water flowed out of the house and into the lake. People who swam in it said it was ice cold. A real estate agent who was an artist built it after he moved here from Cleveland in 1925."

"Did Mr. Tupper live here?" Barb asked.

"Nope. He bought it for one of his top executives, a single mom and entrepreneur named Brownie Wise, who invented the successful Tupperware home parties here in Florida and spread them across the nation and around the world. They called her one of the pioneering women of American business, and she was the first woman ever to appear on the cover of *Business Week*. When she moved into the house in late 1952, she called it *Water's Edge*. She would host huge Tupperware parties for saleswomen from around the country."

As we walked closer, I noted, "It looks dilapidated and abandoned."

"It is," Kevin explained. "In July of 1957, Brownie hosted a luau for twelve hundred guests on the island right out there in the middle of the lake. Unfortunately, a torrential thunderstorm with horrible winds caused severe injuries to twenty-one people. Several almost drowned trying to escape. It was a terrible disaster. As a result, Earl Tupper fired her, and she and her son had to leave the mansion. The house has been empty since because of a ton of litigation. Once people started breaking into the building, they hired a caretaker to live in that mobile home they moved in next to the mansion."

The couple who watched the Tupper Mansion allowed our family to walk the property and picnic on their beach whenever we wanted. Wildlife abounded. Osceola turkeys were frequent guests in our yard and garden along with a pair of sandhill cranes that visited daily. A stunning variety of other birds visited our birdbath and feeders. Even a rare fox or bobcat would trot by. All of the neighborhood residents welcomed us with open arms.[1]

Although our new house was only a short drive from downtown Kissimmee, it was close enough to the country to feel like home. Barb loved her new nest and quickly went about decorating and arranging it into a comfortable and welcoming abode. We loved everything about our home. "The only thing I don't like, Walt," Barb confided to me one evening when I arrived home after supper, "is that you're at work so long. I wish you had more time for our family."

She had inadvertently torn off a painful scab, and my internal conflict began again. *Told you you're spending too much time at work building your practice,* said my nemesis. *A good husband would invest time with his family.*

But, I thought, *a good husband provides for his family. Doesn't the Bible say, "Anyone who does not provide for their relatives, and especially for their own household, has denied the faith and is worse than an unbeliever"?*[2]

The other side countered, *"No one can serve two masters. Either you will hate the one and love the other, or you will be devoted to the one and despise the other. You cannot serve both God and money."*[3]

I shushed them both. Right now, I was too consumed with building a practice and serving my staff and patients with competence and compassion. *After all,* I thought, *doesn't Scripture tell me to "do nothing out of selfish ambition or vain conceit. Rather, in humility value others above yourselves, not looking to your own interests but each of you to the interests of the others"?*[4]

I knew my old self was innately stained by pride and lust, while my new heart longed for humility and fruitfulness. However, if I celebrated not having pride, I was proud, and if I thought myself humble, I was not. One thing I knew for sure: finding a balance was going to be a struggle.

In the meantime, when I was home, using the outdoor grill and hot tub became favorite family activities. And after the kids were asleep, Barb and I would often sneak into the tub's comforting bubbles for relaxation, conversation, and occasional romance. We agreed our home needed a larger family.

So it wasn't a total shock the day Judy grabbed me in the hallway. "Dr. John wants you in room 1."

When I knocked and walked in, John and Barb were talking. "What's up?" I asked.

"Barb wanted me to do a checkup. Since you lost a baby to miscarriage up in Bryson City, she wanted to be sure it would be safe to get pregnant again. I've told her I'm sure the miscarriage was from all the pressure and strain. And, fortunately, that's all in the past now."

I sat by Barb, took her hand, and said, "I'm willing to do every-thing I can to help."

John and Barb smiled knowingly at each other.

"You already have," Barb said as she handed me a small plastic wand with a strip of filter paper on one side. It had two bright blue parallel lines.

"Congratulations!" John exclaimed.

"A baby?" was all I could mutter.

"Children are a heritage from the LORD, offspring a reward from him," John said, quoting a psalm. "Blessed is the man whose quiver is full of them."[5]

Barb and I embraced as the exam room door flew open. Judy, Jean, and Susan burst in, playing "For He's a Jolly Good Fellow" on kazoos.

16

Brother Bill

AS A YOUNG PHYSICIAN, wet-behind-the-ears businessman, and an outsider to the area, I recognized early on the need to have a mentor guide and coach me as an inexperienced Christian, husband, father, professional, and Floridian. In particular, I needed some instruction in balancing the demands and calling of work and home life.

I asked folks I met if they could name a local business leader and family man whose character, integrity, and business skills would most mirror biblical principles. After three well-respected individuals all named the same person, I called him up.

Bryan William Judge Jr. was a second-generation Florida cattleman who spent his childhood on his parents' dairy farm near the tiny hamlet of Holopaw in Osceola County, where he and his father milked forty cows by hand twice a day. He once quipped, "I know the Lord blessed me. I had good parents who spanked me when I had to be spanked and loved me when I had to be loved."

After Mr. Judge graduated with a bachelor's in dairy science from the University of Florida in 1952, the family purchased six hundred acres closer to Kissimmee to increase the herd to one thousand head. As a young man, he was *Outstanding Young Farmer in Florida.* He was an early pioneer in establishing Florida dairy cooperatives, thus becoming a legend in dairy product production, serving for five years as president of the American Dairy Association, becoming Florida Dairyman of the Year, and finally, being inducted into the Dairy Hall of Fame. He and his wife of thirty-five years, Jane, had raised and married off five beautiful daughters. He was an elder at his church and active in international mission work, serving on what was then known as the Foreign Mission Board of the Southern Baptist Convention. Also, Mr. Judge served as a mentor for his five sons-in-law and scores of young businessmen, seminary students, 4-H Club members, and pastors. He went by Bill to most of his friends, but folks in church circles often referred to him as Brother Bill.

I called him out of the blue one evening and explained what I wanted. He told me he'd be willing to meet with me once and see if there might be a potential fit, and he suggested we meet the next Tuesday at 5:30 a.m. at Joanie's Diner downtown.

I arrived in the morning twilight and parked my truck on a side street just around the corner. To my surprise, secured by their reins to the hitching post outside the Saddle Rack Western Store next to an oval galvanized horse trough filled with crystal-clear water were four handsome horses. I stopped to admire the stock and their attractive hand-tooled saddles. They paid me no mind and appeared content, munching on the hay placed at their feet.

I walked around the corner as a cool dawn breeze wafted down Broadway Avenue, carrying the unmistakable aromas of breakfast. As I entered the diner's front door, country music playing from a radio behind the counter set the tone. Perched on barstools were four men in cowboy boots, Wrangler jeans, plaid Western-style shirts characterized by traditional pearl snap buttons, and iconic Stetson hats. I suspected these were the riders of the horses around the corner. A middle-aged, somewhat stout woman standing behind the bar said to me, "Welcome, I'm Joanie. This is my place. Have a seat wherever you want."

Behind her, through a pass-through window from which heating lamps hung, I could see a pair of cooks hard at work in the small kitchen. The smell of bacon and sausage permeated the atmosphere. It felt like home—maybe even better than home—as it reminded me of thirty years earlier when my dad took me to Bob Price's Rexall Drug Store for breakfast at a similar-looking counter in my hometown of Baton Rouge. Warm, comfortable memories washed over me. It was there that my father allowed me to order coffee for the first time—a sure sign of welcoming me to manhood—at age five or six. I remembered feeling self-conscious as I had to doctor the robust, bitter South Louisiana coffee-chicory mix with cream and sugar.

To my right was a table where ten men of various ages and sizes sat. Their smiles and laughter indicated they knew each other well. What appeared to be businessmen deep in conversation occupied a few other tables. *They sure get started early here!* I thought.

Scattered on the table in front of them were half-empty coffee cups, plates overflowing with eggs, bacon, and hash browns, and platters of made-from-scratch biscuits and sausage gravy. I realized I was in breakfast heaven.

I didn't see a single older man anywhere and began looking for a quiet open table.

I walked into the less-crowded and quieter side room, which had square tables that sat four, surrounded by booths along the walls, each with two pressure-formed wood-grain Formica benches. All the tables sported red-and-white-check vinyl tablecloths. I chose a booth and examined the plastic menus and ceramic coffee mugs, both splattered with advertisements from local businesses.

A pleasant surprise was seeing grits on the menu—a breakfast side that Barb and I both loved, especially when prepared with a bit of heavy cream and then slathered with butter and covered with cheese. "Heaven in a bowl," she would say, adding with a laugh, "You know, GRITS stands for Girls Raised in the South." Any cold, cloudy, drizzly South Louisiana day instantly brightened with grits at breakfast. Even today, Barb will see the snow falling outside our Colorado home and exclaim, "It looks like a grits morning today!"

A delicacy in my home growing up was shrimp and grits. Compatible couples could be heard to say, "We go together like shrimp and grits." They are *that* good. When commenting to my three brothers and me about how things didn't always work out as we wanted, our childhood housekeeper, Lena, would say, "Life ain't always going to be shrimp and grits on Easter!"

"Coffee, honey?" A plump but pleasant waitress interrupted my warm memories. I nodded and pushed my mug toward her.

"Hope caffeinated is okay 'cause it's all I've got this morning. Creamer and sugar are there on the table. Are ya waiting for someone?"

"He is," said an older man, who walked up and slid into the bench across from me. He was taller and thinner than I expected. He wore jeans, a well-worn striped, button-down work shirt, and a straw hat with a wide brown band. His farmer's boots had seen a few miles and carried traces of his pasture. His face was thin, tanned, and sun-creased, his eyes narrow set, and his nose prominent and slim, just above a welcoming ear-to-ear smile. He took off his hat and stuck out a sun-browned hand and shook mine with a firm grip. "Are you the physician with whom I'm expecting to meet?" he said, laughing. "It's good to meet you, Dr. Larimore."

"Walt will be fine," I said.

He nodded.

"Good morning, Mr. Judge. Your usual orange juice?"

"Yes, Mildred. Thank you."

After ordering our breakfasts, we each shared our faith stories. I explained that Barb's family attended a Methodist church while I had grown up in the Episcopal chapel at LSU, where my father was an instructor. But neither Barb nor I knew someone could have a personal connection with God until our college years—before then, church was an expected weekly religious formality for us. In college, we both chose to become followers of Jesus.

107

Our spirituality became both real and life-changing—it instantly turned from tedious, prescribed services into a thrilling personal relationship. Bill said his and Jane's walk with Jesus didn't begin until after they were married, had kids, and had established their dairy business in Kissimmee.

After we had eaten, Bill, as he asked me to address him, announced he'd be willing to consider a mentoring relationship with me. The unexpected announcement delighted me, at least for a moment, until he began to share the price of admission.

"Walt," he began, "I suggest we structure our time this way: we'll meet here every Tuesday morning that we're both in town and available—understanding that emergencies happen—from five thirty to seven. My milking's finished by then. Will that give you enough time afterward to see your hospital patients and get to your office on time?"

I nodded.

"Although the subject of the week will vary based on what's going on in our lives, I'd like us to follow this outline, at least initially: the first Tuesday of each month, you'll bring your schedule for us to review. I want you to account to me how you steward your time, how you invest it. I believe a husband and father should give a maximum of fifty hours a week for producing income—and the closer to forty, the better."

I'm sure he saw my eyebrows rise, but he continued, "The second Tuesday of each month, you'll bring your monthly credit card bill and checkbook register. I'll expect you to account to me for how you manage your treasure, your income, and your investments. I want to see how and where you spend, tithe, save, and invest. We'll go over things line by line. We'll talk about budgets and frugality. I believe that financial wealth is not how much money you make but the difference between what you make and what you spend."

Now I know my face was both flushing and showing surprise. This was getting far more detailed and personal than I had planned for or desired.

"We'll devote the third Tuesday to fathering. We'll talk about Kate and Scott. I'd like your permission to drop by and visit with them or to call and talk to them a few days before we meet. I'll inquire of them what sort of daddy you've been."

It felt like beads of sweat broke out on my forehead. Kate and Scott would look forward to that call. In a moment of frustration, I could only imagine one of them saying, "You just wait until Mr. Judge calls!"

"The fourth Tuesday we'll devote to your wife—to how you're providing for, pastoring, protecting, and pursuing her. We'll look at how you are nurturing, nourishing, cherishing, and loving her. Sometimes what I'm oblivious to is obvious to Jane. I want to help you with any blind spots you might have or develop."

I'm sure I looked like a deer in the headlights by the time he finished.

He smiled. "But that's not all. When there's a fifth Tuesday—so four times a year—I want your permission to talk to your partner, Dr. Hartman, and your staff. Their feedback on you as a partner and an employer will be helpful to me in coaching you."

As I began to hyperventilate, my coarser side sneered, *Bet this was not your idea of mentoring and coaching, was it? A process so personal and requiring so much transparency and vulnerability? Must be very threatening! Just tell him no! He'll only learn what a fake you are!*

My better side responded, *Although Bill is not an academician or theologian, you have it on good authority that as a lifelong man of the land and longtime student of the Bible, etched into his soul are the eternal principles of practical theology and living the right way each day.*

Before my harsher side could answer, the better side added, *Remember the pastor who told you Bill Judge is the most Christlike man he knows? He said Bill is the most moral, good, upright, honest, and honorable man he has ever met. Isn't this precisely the mentor you need?*

Bill interrupted my anxious thoughts. "Before you decide, Walt, I have one more requirement."

I wasn't sure I was ready for or could even stand one more item.

"I want to help you with Scripture memory. We'll pick some verses from time to time that will help us as businessmen, husbands, and fathers. Would that be okay?"

Taking a moment to consider his offer and hoping that I could trust him, I nodded my head.

"I liken my mentoring process to a self-cleaning oven. It allows the Holy Spirit to winnow potential mentees to blow away chaff from the grain. Those not truly interested in spiritual maturity just won't last. It's not meant to be easy, but I promise you it will be centered on God and his holy Word. I've always said that the journey of following Jesus isn't easy, but the rewards are worthwhile and eternal. Nevertheless, if it's too much for now, just say so."

"When do you want to start?" I asked.

"What about next week? I'm in town. Are you?"

I nodded.

"I'll see you then. And since that's the second Tuesday of the month, let's go over credit card bills and check registers, okay?"

I took a deep breath as my lousy side sniggered and predicted, *You'll be sorry.*

As was to become his habit, Bill closed our time in a short but heartfelt prayer. We walked out of Joanie's to Conway Twitty's voice coming from the radio singing, "So don't call him a cowboy until you've seen him ride."[1]

Looking at the men in Stetsons as we left, I hoped Bill wouldn't say of me, as the cowboys said of folks who were full of big talk but had no substance or who were fakers or pretenders who couldn't back up their words with actions: "They are all hat and no cattle." Or as folks in South Louisiana might quip, "All vine, no tater."

I had hoped my mentoring with Bill would provide a brain to pick, a shoulder to lean on, and a thrust in the right direction. But it now looked like it was going to be a brain to pick, a shoulder to lean on, and a well-deserved kick in the pants![2]

17

Practical Advice

THE WEEK SEEMED to go by like molasses. Every day I worried more and more about how Bill would judge my financial indiscretions. We were not wealthy or wasteful, but as my more critical side was happy to point out, Barb and I didn't save, invest, or give to the church or charities as we knew we should. And we didn't have the best budgeting system in the world. *Oh well*, my good side thought, *at least he'll have a lot of material to work with!* The other side sneered, *He'll learn you're a fraud!*

I didn't sleep well the night before my first meeting with Bill, and I woke up a good hour before the alarm was to go off with my critical side reminding me that I was about to face criticism and rejection. *When he finds out your poor stewardship habits, he'll drop you like a rock.*

You know you shouldn't worry, my better side said. *He's a good man and will teach you a lot.*

I arrived at Joanie's first, a notebook of Visa statements and a check register in hand. I needed a few minutes alone to calm myself before the coming interaction.

Bill arrived on time, greeted me, and we ordered our breakfasts. After our meal, Bill began—but not at all as I expected. He picked up a notebook he had placed on the seat. "I've found that this level of mentoring can intimidate young men. So I thought we'd use today to let you review my credit card bill and my business and personal check registers. I want to see if you have any suggestions for me. And I want to show you some principles and practices Jane and I have developed over the last thirty years or so. Would that be okay?"

I'm sure my relief must have been palpable, but I could only stammer, "Sure!"

Before our next Tuesday meeting, Bill had me call his daughters and talk to each one. The girls all had some wonderful things to tell me, not knowing they were at the same time teaching me. The Tuesday after that, the fourth of the month, my assignment was to call and talk to Jane about Bill's skills and practices as a husband. That discussion was a precious lesson for me. I just wish I had taped it. The next week, the first of the next month, he brought in his schedule, and we talked a long while about time priorities and how he invested and balanced his time in work, family, church, and community activities.

I wasn't sure why Bill had taken me on, but it pleased me to no end to be on this quest with him. To my family's, my patients', and my everlasting benefit, he coached, discipled, mentored, tutored, and invested in a hardheaded, hot-blooded, inexperienced family man, physician, and small business proprietor who was very young and immature in his spiritual odyssey. Humility and transparency characterized Bill's way of working with me. He never asked me to do anything he wasn't willing to do himself. His relationship with God was honest, vibrant, and fresh. I quickly came to trust, respect, and admire this wise saint. I knew I was in for a remarkable ride as his mentee. Oh, I had no delusions about the work ahead, but I was excited to get started.

There are plenty of biblical examples of mentoring: Jethro mentored Moses, who mentored Joshua, who mentored leaders in his army. Eli mentored Samuel, who mentored David, who mentored

Solomon. Elijah mentored Elisha, who mentored King Jehoash. In the New Testament, Jesus mentored the twelve apostles, who established the Christian church by mentoring hundreds of other leaders, including Paul, who mentored Timothy, who mentored "faithful men" such as Epaphras. Priscilla and Aquila mentored Apollos. The list goes on and on, but all followed Paul's pastoral admonition to Timothy to train other people who will then mentor others.[1] Men mentoring men and women mentoring women—that's how the church began and spread. It's the same today.

Make no mistake, one-on-one relationships are costly and time-consuming. And the difficult work of building a relationship doesn't start in a church structure. It begins at places like Joanie's Diner everywhere. And this extraordinary relationship, which began in 1985, continues yet today—thirty-five years later.

Barb and I always discussed what Bill was teaching me. He had encouraged us to be good managers of what he called the *4 Ts of stewardship*—the care and management of God's gifts to us—including our temple, time, talents, and treasure. By *temple*, Bill meant our physical bodies, as in the "temple of the Holy Spirit."[2] One of our first applications was to become better stewards of our treasure, our money, by continuing to tithe but also by starting to build up an emergency fund that would represent six months of expenses. In addition, we decided it was time to begin to invest for our retirement years.

Bill taught that recognizing future needs and making arrangements for them are biblically astute practices. He used the example of Joseph to illustrate the wisdom of saving. In Genesis 41, Joseph had Egypt store provisions for a famine that was prophesied to come.

He also shared the example of God's command to the Israelites in Exodus 16 to gather manna each morning for that day. The exception was that on Friday they were to gather two days' worth.

Those Jews who went out on the Sabbath to gather manna found none. Bill said, "Their failure to plan and save led to their going hungry."

"But, Bill," I countered, "what about Jesus telling us not to be worried for tomorrow? And what about the parable of the rich fool who had such an abundance that he planned to build a larger barn, and God told him he would die that night?"

"Great questions, Walt. And I'm pleased to see you're using Scripture to determine your thoughts, actions, and plans. It's wise to do so. Let me show you two other verses that have helped me in this area. Look up Proverbs 21:20 and read it to me."

I found it and read out loud, "The wise store up choice food and olive oil, but fools gulp theirs down."

"Flip over to Proverbs 6:6–8. King Solomon uses an insect as an example of the wisdom of saving."

I read, "Go to the ant, you sluggard; consider its ways and be wise! It has no commander, no overseer or ruler, yet it stores its provisions in summer and gathers its food at harvest."

"The real issue, as it *always* is with Jesus, is one of the heart," Bill explained. "I don't believe Jesus was speaking about not saving now for needs in the future. What he was talking about is where we should focus our hearts. We are to value the things that God values, trust in his provision instead of our wealth, and live wisely. Like I always say, the heart of the matter is usually a matter of the heart."

Barb and I talked to several acquaintances who suggested a Christian financial advisor in a nearby town. We made an appointment, and after we interviewed him and he looked over our financial records, he recommended a particular investment for us. It was a tax-exempt investment, but very expensive. Even so, I was excited about it and its potential. On the way home, I asked Barb what she thought.

"Walt, I don't like it."

Her response surprised me, and I asked, "Why not?"

"I don't know. It just doesn't feel right for us—at least to me."

I figured she just didn't appreciate the complexity, so I spent some time during our drive explaining it to her.

As I drove up to our home, Barb said, "I don't know why, but I just don't think we should."

I thought she was saying, "I do not understand this investment." So I spent extra time at our kitchen table with the charts and graphs and data from the prospectus trying to convince her why this was the correct security for us. It made perfect sense to me.

When I finished, Barb said, "I know you think this is the right deal for us. And I understand what you are saying, I do, but all I can see are red flags."

"You don't trust me?" was all I could say. I felt stabbed in the back by her lack of confidence.

She reached out and touched my arm softly. "Walt, I admire your intellect, recognize your risk-taking nature, and trust God is leading you in this. So although I don't think it's a good idea, I'll leave the decision to you."

I was relieved to know she had confidence in my financial acumen and spirituality. Unfortunately, on both accounts, I came up far shorter than I ever could have imagined.

18

Little Ones

BESIDES KEEPING MY PRACTICE YOUTHFUL, the children I cared for kept me young as well. I walked into an examination room where a young patient, Erin, and her mother were waiting.

"Dr. Walt," she said, "I've got the chicken pops," referring to her obvious case of chicken pox. In those days, almost ten years before the chicken pox vaccine was released, it was a highly contagious viral disease that caused between 250 and 500 itchy blisters across the body and even inside the mouth. Each year about four million people got the disease, over ten thousand were hospitalized, and over one hundred died. Fortunately, it was mild for most people.

"Well, how are you feeling?" I asked.

She looked very serious and responded, "I have a very, *very* high temperature."

I wasn't surprised since fever, loss of appetite, and fatigue were common with chicken pox, so I asked, "How high has your temperature been?"

"Three hundred and three degrees," she replied.

A very surprised me replied, "Well, that *is* a very, very high temperature."

She crossed her arms and nodded while responding, "I told you so!"

I saw this same little girl a few months later for a well-child visit, just after she started first grade. When I asked how she was doing, she and her mother giggled, explaining: "After the initial week of school, Erin's teacher called to tell me that every morning when the children stood to say the Pledge of Allegiance, Erin refused to take part. I expressed my concern, and I asked Erin about it when she got home." She looked down at her daughter. "Tell Dr. Walt what you told me."

Erin smiled and blushed. "I said I didn't want to apologize to the flag."

"Well," I said, laughing, "I think an ear and hearing check is in order today." It did not surprise me that she had a wax buildup in each ear that Judy was able to wash out using a Waterpik.

At another office visit, she was wearing an embroidered Minnie Mouse shirt after returning from a birthday party at Disney World.

"Erin," I exclaimed as I walked into the room, "I *love* your T-shirt!"

"Thank you, Dr. Walt," she replied, blushing and smiling.

"Can I have it?" I inquired.

Without a second's pause, she blurted, "No!"

"Why not?" I asked.

She responded, "Because you're too fat!"

Her mother came to the rescue. "Oh, honey, he's not *that* fat!"

This vivacious youngster generated what became the only complaint ever filed against my medical license. I received notice via certified mail that an accusation had been investigated. They determined I had done no wrong, and the case was closed. It listed a number I could call for more details. I called the attorney for the Board of Medicine. To my surprise, when she got on the phone, she was laughing.

"Oh, Dr. Larimore," she began. "This is *so* funny."

To me, it was not amusing!

"We received a complaint from a little girl whose mother is a nurse at a hospital down there."

I immediately suspected to whom she was referring.

"It turns out that the state of Florida sent out notices to all health professionals, encouraging them to notify them anonymously if they saw potential malpractice or unethical behavior by another health professional. The intent is to weed out the bad apples from the system."

"What was the complaint against me?"

The attorney chuckled. "It turns out the girl's mother received her notice at home. She left it out, and her young daughter read it one evening after you had seen her. You had administered two vaccine shots to her, and she was reporting you for the needle sticks."

"And the grievance was what?"

"Pain and discomfort," she responded, now laughing hilariously. I didn't find it funny at all.

"Well, we had to investigate. State law requires it. Her mother was apoplectic. She wanted to call you and apologize. I had to tell her not to, given this is an anonymous process. The case is closed from our viewpoint and expunged from our system. Nothing will be in our records, and we won't have to report this to the National Practitioner Data Bank."

A chill went down my spine. The NPDB had just launched that year and was a web-based archive of reports containing information on medical malpractice payments and adverse actions related to health-care professionals. Congress had established it to prevent unscrupulous practitioners from moving state to state without disclosure or discovery of previous damaging performance. The idea was to promote quality health care and deter fraud and abuse within health-care delivery systems. But clinicians viewed it with great suspicion.

"Well, I'm glad to hear that!" was all I could think to mutter.

"I talked to the little girl, and she's a cutie. You've got a live wire of a patient there, doctor."

I could finally chuckle. "Yes, that I do!"

John and I always encouraged the young mothers in our practice to breastfeed, and we then supported them as they did so. Barb and Cleta, who taught our prenatal classes, also strongly advocated for breastfeeding. In addition, it was essential to prepare the parents with an older child or children at home for the probability of sibling rivalry.

At one well-child visit of a four-year-old boy, John entered the exam room to find the child's mother breastfeeding her new daughter, whose four-year-old brother was sulking in the adjoining chair.

John encouraged her to continue breastfeeding and turned his attention to the older brother. "You look mad," he observed.

"Well, Dr. John," he responded, "I am!"

"Do you want to tell me about it?" John asked, his curiosity aroused.

The little boy furrowed his eyebrows as he planned his answer. "Well, I'm mad that my mom won't let me share my hot dog with my little sister."

The mom appeared surprised, learning of her son's feelings for the first time, and with a gentle, reassuring smile said, "Oh, honey, we can't feed your sister a hot dog yet—"

But before she could finish, her very observant son retorted, "Well, why not? You let her eat your breast!"

The mother looked shocked while John stifled a chuckle.

When my truck was in the shop, we had only one vehicle. So after making early rounds at the hospital, I'd come home, and we would all load up in the minivan. We'd drop Kate off at elementary school, and after dropping me off at the office, Barb would drive past Rose Hill Cemetery. Scott, secure in his car seat, would start yelling, "Mommy! Jesus and the sheep! Jesus and the sheep!"

"What did you see?" Barb would ask.

"Jesus and the sheep!" he'd exclaim.

"Where?"

"There!" he'd answer, pointing to the cemetery.

Seeing nothing but trees and tombstones, she would ask, "Scott, what are you talking about?"

He could only point to the cemetery as they zipped by.

One day after work, when I walked in and kissed Barb, she was giggling. "What's so funny?" I asked.

"Today, I was driving alongside the cemetery. The traffic backed up, and I was just creeping along. I glanced to the side and noticed a road leading into the middle of the cemetery. And guess what I saw?" she asked, chuckling.

"I have no idea."

"In the center of the cemetery, there's a statue of Jesus surrounded by several sheep. So Scott wasn't kidding or crazy!"

In Bryson City, our children had lost their innocence; however, they were now recovering better than we ever thought possible. They both were hopeful, optimistic, curious, and full of questions. They loved learning, at least in the subjects in which they were interested. They were kind, generous, lighthearted, and playful. They were like most little ones—in other words, they were everything we adults often wish we were still.

19

Carpe Duh!

RON WAS A WIDOWER and a terrific father with three daughters all under the age of eight, and he cared for them as a single dad. His in-laws lived in town and assisted with raising the rambunctious girls, but even in the best of circumstances, being a single parent is one of the toughest jobs on earth.

He brought in his youngest, Sally, to see me with a small infected area on her cheek. Facial infections can become dangerous if they invade the tissues around the eye. From there, they can spread to the brain in a matter of hours. If a parent called in with a child with an eye or facial infection, we saw them immediately.

The little girl looked healthy other than the small area of cellulitis on her cheek. There was no boil or pimple to lance, and there was no infection around the eye, what we call *periorbital cellulitis*. I pulled out a prescription pad. "Here's an antibiotic. It's one teaspoon three times a day for a week. You should see improvement in twenty-four hours. If not, or if there's any worsening, call right away, okay?"

The next day it alarmed me to see Sally on my schedule. When I walked into the exam room, her cheek appeared much worse.

There was still no boil or sign of infection in the periorbital tissues, but the cellulitis involved most of the cheek, which felt hot and looked fiery red.

"Any fever or change in activity or appetite?" I asked, exploring for any suggestion that it was spreading into her bloodstream.

"Nope. She's acting normal. It's just that it *looks* so much worse."

"I agree." I knew I didn't need to ask, given how compliant a father he was, but I wanted to be sure. "Did you get the antibiotic?"

"Yes. I picked it up right after the visit with you yesterday. Administered three doses yesterday and one this morning. But it's not working very well."

I nodded in agreement. "I think we need to give an injection of an antibiotic and change to a stronger oral antibiotic."

Ron nodded and added, "I agree. The one you prescribed is just too hard to use."

I thought his statement was unusual. "In what way?"

"Well, the directions said one teaspoon three times a day. So I pour the liquid into a teaspoon, but when I put it on the infection, it just runs off her face."

I'm sure my eyes revealed my surprise. Ron looked stunned. "Oh, my goodness!" he muttered. "It's not a topical medicine, is it?"

"No, sir!" I answered as we both laughed. Fortunately, Sally was no worse for wear, and with the medicine administered correctly, she quickly recovered!

Myra was a young child with a chronic cough. During the process of trying to figure out what was going on, and after several failed treatments, the mother became increasingly impatient—often threatening to take the child to a specialist.

"I'd be more than happy to arrange a consult," I said, "any time you want. But they are going to want to run some basic tests. Let's do those here. It will be faster and cheaper. And if we find out what this is, we're good."

To my relief, we discovered the cause: cough-variant asthma—
a type of asthma in which the child's main symptom is a dry,
nonproductive cough. When the child's tiny bronchioles constrict, instead of causing wheezing, which is usually the case with
asthma, they lead to a cough. I suggested starting the child on a
bronchodilator that was delivered through a small handheld container. The mother was skeptical but agreed to give it a try before
heading out to see another doctor. I offered to have Judy give the
mother instructions on how to use it with a spacing device. The
inhaler is pumped once, releasing the vaporized medication into
the spacer. Then the child can slowly inhale the mist deep into
the lungs.

However, the mother's retort was something like, "Do I look like
I was born yesterday? Of course I know how to use the sprayer!"
I handed her the prescription and recommended a follow-up visit
to retest the child's lungs in a couple of weeks.

At the follow-up, the mother appeared irritated. "We need to
see a specialist!"

"Give me an update. What's going on?"

"You said you'd fix my child's cough, but you didn't. She's no
better. The medication made no difference at all."

"Well, sometimes we have to try one or two inhalers to find
just the right one. But first, how often did you use the inhaler?"

"Every four hours while she is awake. Just as the instructions
on the spray container said. We went through the first one in a
week and got it refilled."

I never had anyone call an inhaler a spray container, I thought.
*And with at least sixty sprays per canister, she must have been using
eight to nine squirts per day.* "Could you be using it incorrectly?" I
asked, almost immediately wishing I had not phrased it that way.
The mother sat up straight and became visibly upset.

"Do you think I'm an imbecile?" she exclaimed.

"No! Not at all," I said. "Maybe it's the inhaler. Can you show
me how you give it to her?"

The mother looked irritated, jerked around, pulled her purse off the floor, grabbed the inhaler out of it, glared at me as she gave it several shakes, yanked off the cover, and turned to her daughter. "Let's show the doctor we're not idiots, sweetheart," she growled. "Lift your chin."

The daughter dutifully looked up at the ceiling and unbuttoned her blouse, as the mother sprayed one spray on each side of her neck, and another on each side of her chest, as one might do with a perfume atomizer. I tried not to laugh and kept a serious face. The little girl coughed, and the mother glowered. "See, it actually makes her worse."

"Maybe we could try a little different approach. Could I show you something?"

The mother looked suspicious but nodded.

I stepped out of the room for two reasons. The first was to have a good chuckle. Big Mrs-know-it-all really didn't! After composing myself, I retrieved a sample spacing device. Back in the room, I took the inhaler, attached it to the device, and actuated the spray into it, which created a little cloud of aerosolized medication.

"Now," I told the girl, "after you breathe out, put your lips on the mouthpiece here, and slowly breathe in the spray."

The mother's eyes widened as she gasped. "Oh, no! You mean the medicine is supposed to go in the lungs and not on the skin?"

She began to laugh hysterically. Between snorts, she blurted out, "No wonder it didn't work! I feel like an idiot!! Carpe duh!"

Used correctly, the medication worked perfectly!

At home, we found out we didn't know as much about caring for our children as we first thought. Kate was our compliant child. Raising her made us feel like the most competent and equipped parents in history. I thought I should write Dr. James Dobson at Focus on the Family, as he was called *America's Foremost Family Counselor*,[1] and suggest he have Barb and me on his nationally syndicated radio program so we could teach others our amazing skills.

Then, along came Scott. Independent, strong-willed, autonomous, free-spirited. I remember the day I first recognized his iron-willed side while we were still living in North Carolina. I was watching a football game on our brand-new console TV. Those were cathode-ray tube televisions contained in a wooden cabinet that looked like furniture.

Scott, wearing only a diaper, began to crawl over to the TV. He pulled himself up to a standing position and reached for the on-off button. As he did, he turned to face me.

"Don't turn it off," I warned.

His hand reached closer to the knob.

"Son, I will not tell you again. Don't you dare."

He smiled, I think it may have been a spiteful grin if such a thing is possible in a toddler, swung his hand, and punched the knob off. He looked back with a defiant look as if to say, "What are you going to do about that?"

Bold-faced defiance of authority? Well, we had a brief discussion followed by a short session of discipline. As he cried, I scooped him up on my lap. "I love you, son. Nothing you can do can make me love you less. But when you are deliberately disobedient with either your mother or me, there will be consequences. Understand?"

He nodded, and I gave him a hug and a kiss.

On another Saturday, this time in Kissimmee, I was again watching a football game on TV. The doorbell rang, and Scott ran from his room, yelling, "I'll get it." He ran to the door, looked out through the sidelight, and said, "No need to get that. It's nothing."

The doorbell rang again.

"It's no one!" he exclaimed, pressing his back to the door.

Curious *and* suspicious, I walked to the door and opened it. There, to my surprise, stood Officer Gib Michaels, his cruiser parked in the driveway.

"Dr. Larimore, did someone call 9-1-1?" he asked.

"It wasn't me!" Scott said.

Gib seemed amused and knelt. "Then that someone hung up on the 9-1-1 operator without saying a word. They sent me to investigate. Is there any problem here, sir?"

Barb walked up behind me.

"Ma'am, any problem?"

"There may be, Officer." She looked at Scott. "Scott, did you call 9-1-1?"

Scott looked down, in noticeable embarrassment. He nodded.

Gib smiled and stood. "Dr. and Mrs. Larimore, I'll take Scott to the cruiser and talk with him. Would that be okay? It won't take long."

Barb and I both nodded. Scott whimpered as Gib led him away. We watched as Gib sat Scott in the driver's seat of the cruiser and knelt next to him. They spoke for a few minutes. He had Scott put on his hat, talk into the radio, and even turn on the flashing lights. Scott hopped out of the car and stood at attention. Office Michaels placed something on his shirt and also stood at attention as he and Scott saluted each other. They walked back to the house.

Scott exclaimed, "Look, Dad! I've got a badge. I'm an official City of Kissimmee junior policeman!"

"Doc," Gib explained. "We had a heart-to-heart. I think your son understands what he did wrong. I don't think I'll need to arrest him or take him to the lockup. After talking to him, we radioed into dispatch, and he apologized to our dispatch officer and promised not to disturb them with a prank call in the future. Right, Scott?"

Scott saluted. "Yes, sir!"

"Furthermore, I've commissioned him a junior officer with the Kissimmee Police Department."

"Are you sure he's qualified after this crime?" I asked.

"Yes, sir," Gib said. "I think he's both repentant and rehabilitated.

I think he'll be a fine representative of our department." He looked down. "You won't let me down, will you, Scott?"

"No, sir!"

"Thanks, Officer," I said.

He smiled from ear to ear. "This makes my day, Doc!"

"Ours too," Barb said.

20

The Menace

ONE SUNDAY AFTERNOON, Scott and one of his neighborhood friends, Cameron, ran into the house.

"Dad, we need your help. Cinderella went up the chimney!"

Kate and Scott had just adopted two rescue cats. He named his Ebenezer Sneezer, and she called hers Cinderella.

"How'd she do that?"

They took me to the back porch and pointed to the outdoor stucco grill, which was built into the wall and shared a chimney with the fireplace in our sitting room. "She jumped up onto the chair, then the grill, and climbed into the chimney. I guess the flue was open."

I could hear the pitiful meows echoing in the chimney.

"Cameron and I went on the roof and took off the chimney cap. There's more than enough room for me to get down, but I didn't because I wasn't sure I could get back up by myself."

"I was going to get a rope and let him down," Cameron explained. "But I wasn't sure I was strong enough to pull him up. Can you try, Dr. Larimore?"

I thought, *How'd you get on the roof in the first place? How'd you get the chimney cap off? Why didn't you just reach up into the flue and pull her out?* Cameron answered my unspoken questions.

"We tried reaching up into the chimney to get her, but she jumped up on a ledge, and we can't reach her."

I leaned over the grill, peered up the chimney, confirming his observation.

"We thought about pouring a bucket of water down the chimney from the roof to drive her out, but with our luck, either the water would splash into the living room, or the wet cat would run through the house making marks on Mom's new carpet," Scott explained.

"Good thinking," I said, as I shuddered even thinking about the mess the cat would make—and remembering when Scott, as a young toddler, had taken Barb's new lipstick and drawn a picture for her on the brand-spanking-new cornflower-blue bedroom carpet. That scene was *not* a pretty sight. *Maybe he's learning,* I thought.

I closed the flue going to the living room, leaving the outside grill flue open. We grabbed three pairs of gloves and a rope from the garage. I assigned Cameron the job of staying on the back porch and closing the flue once Cinderella was out. Scott and I climbed the ladder they had leaned against the back of the house and up onto the flat asphalt roof of the porch. The brick chimney rose about three feet above the roof. Looking down, there appeared to be more than enough room. Since he was wearing old, beat-up clothes, the ash and soot stains would not be too much of a problem.

"So," I asked, "do you want to go down headfirst and be able to hold Cinderella as I pull you up, or do you want to go down feet first and use your feet to scoot her out of the chimney?"

Scott thought a moment and said, "If I go feet first and somehow the knot comes undone, or you drop me, that'll be safer."

"I think that's a good plan." And it was. After grabbing two old towels to wrap around the rope for padding, I put it around his chest and tied what I consider the most useful knot in the world, a bowline knot. It won't slip when in use and comes undone easily even after being tightened under weighty loads. And it wouldn't constrict Scott's chest.

I was lowering Scott inch by inch, when I heard Barb yell from the yard, "What are you doing up there, Walt?"

"He's lowering Scott down the chimney," Cameron responded.

"What! Why?"

"Kate's cat is stuck in the chimney," Cameron answered.

Scott yelled, "She's off the ledge."

"I've got her," Cameron yelled from the porch. "She's out."

I pulled Scott up and out. His grin spread from ear to ear. "We did it!" he exclaimed as we exchanged a high five.

As the kids were putting away the ladder, gloves, and rope, Barb glared at me. "You didn't have to do *that*!"

"Why not?"

"Two reasons. One, if we had put food on the grill, she would have come out when she got hungry. Two, what if one of our neighbors had seen you sending *your* child down the chimney?"

She made good points. "But it *was* a fun adventure," I said meekly.

"Well, you and the boys will have another fun adventure now."

"Which is?"

"You need to wash that cat and the back porch. I want it spotless, you hear?"

I nodded. But my difficulties did not end there. That night, I put Scott to bed, read a bedtime Bible story, said a quick prayer, and kissed him goodnight.

"Dad," he said, "we sure had a fun day, didn't we?"

"We did," I said, "even though Cinderella did *not* like her bath." We both had several Band-Aids on our arms from cat scratches.

Scott furrowed his brow. "I just have one question. I could barely fit down the chimney. How in the world is Santa going to get down it this Christmas?"

"Morning sickness" was a common problem among our pregnant patients; however, it's misnamed. In about only one-third of women does it occur in the morning. For another third, it's in the afternoon or evening. In the third group, in which Barb firmly resided, it lasted all day long. Fortunately, the nausea was significantly blunted with a combination of staying hydrated, resting often, and taking ginger capsules, vitamin B_6, and the antihistamine doxylamine, all while wearing an acupressure Sea-Band on her wrist.

One afternoon, she was in her bedroom with the door closed, talking on the phone with a friend. The kids knew that the closed door meant privacy was desired. They could not enter without knocking, and then only if it was an emergency. Scott understood the first two but didn't always do so well with number three.

There were several thuds on the door. "Mom. Mom!" Scott called out.

"I'm on the phone, Scott. You'll have to wait."

Several sharp knocks were followed with Scott exclaiming, "Mom! Mom! Quick!"

Barb walked to the door and cracked it open. "Scott, I'm on the phone. When I'm done, I'll come out. You need to remember that patience is waiting without fussing." She shut the door and went back to her conversation.

The door shook with several sharp wraps, and a frantic Scott yelled, "Mom! The kitchen's on fire!"

Barb dropped the phone, yanked the door open, and sprinted to the smoky kitchen. As she entered, the smoke alarm began to blare. The microwave door was closed, but she could see flames through the glass door, and smoke was pouring out. She had the presence of mind to turn off the microwave and then grab our small fire extinguisher from under the sink, pull its pin, throw open the microwave oven door, and spray the base of the fire to douse the flames.

Barb sat down, relieved but exasperated. Her kitchen was a messy combination of a burned smell, thick smoke, and extinguisher chemicals. In her frustration, she began to sob and yelled, "Scott, what did you do?"

It turns out he had taken a plastic bag of leftover popcorn and was microwaving it as a snack. Unfortunately, it had a twist tie, and the metal in the closure had sparked and begun the fire. Our remorseful son helped his mother and sister air out the house and scrub the kitchen, but for years, Barb could smell the light fragrance of smoke whenever she used the appliance—a reminder of a near disaster averted.

Of course, when I got home, I heard the command that occasionally greeted me when I arrived at home: "*You* need to talk with *your* son!"

21

Iron Will

SCOTT'S STRONG WILL returned another afternoon. I answered the pounding on our front door to find a somewhat perturbed Judge Thacker. Appearing agitated, and not one to mince words, he launched: "Walt, someone cut a flower off my Bird of Paradise plant. It's one of my prize plants, and it was my first bloom of the season. And I emphasize it *was*."

Russell took great pride in his yard and landscaping. He kept them up immaculately. He had proudly shown me several of his newer Bird of Paradise plants just the week before. Their foliage resembled small banana leaves with long petioles. The leaves grow in two ranks to form a fanlike crown of evergreen foliage, which is thick, waxy, and glossy green. It is truly a very attractive ornamental plant that can reach a height of three to four feet.

"Is Scott around? I saw the boy eyeing the blooms. I told him I had been waiting over a year for these young plants to bloom and that when it was ready, I would cut one or two for Edna."

At that moment, the sliding door of the kitchen opened. Scott strode in from the back porch and called, "Dad, where's a flower vase?" He started pulling open cabinet doors with one hand while holding a green stalk with a beautiful bloom at the end in the other. The flower resembled a brightly colored bird in flight, thus its name.

Judge Thacker and I walked to the kitchen.

"Scott, what are you up to?" I asked.

His back was turned to us as he continued his search, banging from one cabinet to another. "Just getting a vase to take this flower to Mrs. Edna."

Russell cleared his throat, and Scott stopped in his tracks, slowly turning around.

"Uh-oh," he whispered.

"Uh-oh, indeed!" Russell answered. "Well, what is done is done. So how about you and I take this over to Mrs. Edna?"

Scott's big blue eyes widened as he smiled and nodded.

"But from now on, I need you to respect my wishes, okay?"

Scott nodded again.

"Let's go."

After a while, Scott ran into the house, yelling as he went to his room, "I need to put on my swimsuit! Judge Thacker's gonna let me clean his pool. It's the sentence for my crime!"

In an instant, he changed and charged through the house, yelling, "Is that okay, Dad?" as he ran out of the house and across the street.

I realized how inadequately equipped I was for this nonstop whirlwind of a youngster whose mischievousness would incessantly burst forth, often camouflaging his heart of gold. If we set a boundary fence, he'd find it and lean against it, pushing with all his might. His nature was to test his mother and me in every way possible. My overinflated image of my fathering skills was soon crushed by the reality of a tornado named Scott.

Instead of instructing Dr. Dobson's audience, we joined it, purchasing *The Strong-Willed Child*. We were so glad to have the wise advice and experience of this Christian father and psychologist and read part of a chapter to each other almost every night.

Of the problematic child, Dr. Dobson wrote, as if addressing us, "Their frustrated parents wonder where they went wrong. . . .

They desperately need a little coaching about what to do next."[1] He reassured us that as challenging as it is to raise a strong-willed child—to balance love and discipline—they can grow up to be incredible people with strong characters if lovingly guided with understanding and the right training. Chapters such as "Shaping the Will," "Protecting the Spirit," and "The Most Common Mistake" were a valuable education and incredible encouragement for us—along with what was to become our favorite piece of parenting advice from the Bible: "You shall not murder."[2]

Raising a strong-willed child is like riding a roller coaster for the first time. You quickly learn there are many ups and downs with unexpected twists and turns. You never know what's coming next. All you can do is hold on, pray during the gyrations, and know that one day it will end—hopefully without crashing!

One summer day, Barb went to pick up Kate and Scott at Vacation Bible School. The receptionist quickly found Kate but could not locate Scott. In fact, they could not find any child named Scott. The director explained, "We don't have any Scotts registered."

It shocked Barb. "You must. I brought him this morning."

"What's the last name?" she asked.

"Larimore."

The woman looked down the list. "We have a Kate Larimore and a Justin Larimore." She looked up and smiled. "Let me go get 'Justin' for you."

"But, Mom," he explained, "I don't like the name Scott! I prefer Justin. So that's what I told them my name was."

Another time, he calmly explained to us that he opened his window each night after bedtime prayers and lights out to let someone enter and stay with him in his room each night.

"What? Who?" Barb asked, shocked.

"Jane," Scott calmly answered as he ate his cereal.

"Jane? Who is Jane, and why do you let her in?"

"Him. Jane's a man," Scott answered matter-of-factly.

"You let a man in your room?"

"Of course. Jane works construction and needs a place to sleep. But don't worry. He only smokes and uses the bathroom outside, sleeps in my closet, and doesn't eat any of our food."

To Barb's relief, Scott explained Jane was a pretend friend. "I just made him up in my head," Scott said. "He's not in real life." He looked at Barb inquisitively and asked, "You don't think I'd let someone in my bedroom at night, do you?"

Barb did not answer him.

Another day I arrived home to find Kate and Barb reading in the family room.

"You need to go see *your* son," Barb barked. Her tone of voice announced I best not inquire of much detail other than, "Where is he?"

"In prison," Kate calmly answered. "His room."

I walked down the hallway, knocked on his door, and heard a muffled voice ask, "Who is it?"

"Dad. May I come in?" Not hearing a negative response, I entered the darkened room. Scott was lying on his bed with his face to the wall. I walked over and sat by him.

"What's the story?"

"Mom and I had a really, really bad and terrible day."

"What happened?"

"We had some disagreements."

"About what?" I thought this discussion would take quite a while.

"Stuff."

"So what happened?"

He turned over and rolled his eyes. "Well, if you *have* to know." He sighed and explained, "She got really, really mad. She then got a suitcase and came in here." He pointed to the suitcase by his dresser.

"And?"

"Well, she packed it and took it and me and Kate to the van.

She made us get in and buckle up, and she drove us down Neptune Road to the Osceola Children's Home."

I couldn't believe what I was hearing. "Where?" I asked in disbelief. "What?! You're kidding?"

He shook his head and rolled back toward the wall. From behind me, Barb, who had walked into the room, explained. "I drove him to the Children's Home. I opened the van door and took out his suitcase and put it on the ground. I asked him to get out and told him he needed to take his stuff and march up to the front door, and he could stay there with foster parents until he decided he could live with and follow our household rules."

My mind was spinning. They *had* to be kidding. But I could see that they were not.

"Scott started sobbing, Daddy," said Kate as she entered the room. "Mom just closed the van door, got back in the van, and began to drive away. Scott was just standing there, crying. It was *so* sad. I began to cry too. Mom drove around the circular driveway and back in front of him. She opened the passenger window and asked Scott if he had anything to say. He told Mom he wanted to go home, and that he loved her so much, and that he would be good forever and ever and ever, Amen."

I'm sure I looked at my wife in disbelief. "And?"

"I told him I needed him to apologize, and he did. I told him I needed him to really, really mean it this time."

"Scott said he did, Daddy. He was telling the truth. The *real* truth," Kate explained. "So Mom told him to get his suitcase and to get back in the van. He did, and we came home."

"I told him he needed to go to his room and spend some quiet time thinking about whether he wanted to live here or somewhere else," Barb said. "I told him that when you got home, we could discuss it further but *not* to unpack his bag until we all worked this out."

Not smelling any aromas hinting at dinner coming from the kitchen, I interjected, "How about this? Let's call a truce, a timeout for dinner, and go to Fat Boy's Barbeque?" Pit-smoked ribs, chicken, and pork, complemented by sweet tea, in a no-frills, family-friendly establishment—it was a perfect place that we often visited as a family to cool off, calm down, mend damaged hearts, soothe sore feelings, and soften iron wills.

At home that evening, I helped my son unpack and tucked him in with a special prayer and hug. We all awoke the next morning refreshed and recommitted to continue together the thrilling roller-coaster ride called life.

PART FOUR

22

First Rodeo

ALICE RAMSEY, AN X-ray technician and a longtime resident of Osceola County, stopped by the office for a quick visit. "Dr. Larimore," she began, "you've done a lot of sports medicine, haven't you?"

I nodded. "Yes. In fact, I trained in family medicine *and* sports medicine at Duke. Why?"

"Have you heard of the Silver Spurs Riding Club?"

"That's the twice-a-year rodeo, right?"

"Well, actually the Riding Club is a social group started by some Osceola County ranchers back in the '40s."

"They staged a Western show on the Partin property to raise money for the war, right?"

"Well, that was in 1944. But at the beginning, in 1941, they were formed to ride their horses in the inaugural parade for a newly elected Florida governor. That appearance drew a lot of attention from the press and resulted in invitations to appear in other events. So the founders decided they would continue to meet and share their common interest in horseback riding and herding cattle. The next few years, they were in parades around the south, including the Orange Bowl Parade down in Miami. Then they became well known for performing square dances on their horses—they called it *Quadrille*. Only then did they decide to hold their first rodeo. It was in a small arena on property donated by Henry O. Partin."

"Actually," I said, "our home on Starfish Street is on that very land."

Alice laughed. "That's right. In fact, rodeos weren't held in the current facility until 1950. Anyway, one of our local radiologists, Hamp Sessions, is in the Silver Spurs and has served as the rodeo doctor for a few years, but he'd be delighted if you'd take it off his hands. He's been happy to do it, but as a radiologist, he doesn't feel very qualified. Would you consider it?"

I was interested and asked Alice what they expected.

"Dr. Sessions and I have organized a first-aid room that's located underneath the spectator stands just next to the livestock chutes. Best seats in the house, if you ask me. We'd want you or Dr. Hartman to be at *each* of the performances. Serious injuries among the riders are not very common, and if they occur, they are first evaluated by the rodeo clowns who are in the arena—well, actually, they now like to be called *bullfighters* and are proud of saying that they are in the cowboy protection business. If the injury is serious, they call the EMTs who are on standby to come into the ring. The EMTs bring the injured competitor to our first-aid room, so we don't have to take any risk entering the ring. You'd assess the damage and decide if it can be treated there or if the cowboy needs to be transported to the hospital. Fortunately, the competitors are pretty tough and seldom come in to see us."

"Do we provide first aid for spectators?"

"The EMTs do that. We're just there for the professionals."

"Do I need to bring anything?"

"Nope," Alice said. "I'll have everything you need, including supplies for splinting, minor procedures, and suturing. The week before the rodeo, I'll go over the supply list with you to see if there's anything else you might need. You'll have special parking next to the arena, and your family is welcome to come sit with you."

I couldn't believe my good fortune. "I'm in!" I told Alice, who beamed in response.

———

The enticing smell of hamburgers and popcorn wafted across the stadium, which held over eight thousand rodeo fans from several states. The crowd was a mixture of cattle and horse folk, who were mostly farmers and ranchers, as well as myriad tourists duded up in their annual rodeo cowboy and cowgirl gear. It wasn't challenging to tell the difference between these groups. I was in the latter group, decked out in my cowboy boots (a gift from Barb's dad during my medical school days), new Wrangler jeans ("true" cowboys only wore Wranglers), a new cowboy shirt with pearl snap buttons, and a Stetson hat—all from Goold's Department Store. Founder Lothar Goold had retired in 1974, and a distant cousin, Harry Lowenstein, a survivor of the Kaiserwald concentration camp, along with his wife, Carol, and son, David, took over. Harry supervised Barb's and my shopping trip.

"We've had five generations of families shop here," Harry told me as he helped me select apparel. "I want you to look local—perhaps a bit rode and worn," he advised, "not starched up like the tourist dudes."

I still felt uncomfortably conspicuous as Alice and her six-year-old son, also named Scott, found and escorted Scott and me to our assigned sitting area just outside of the first-aid room. She then took us under the stands to see the livestock. "They treat 'em better than any animals on the planet," she explained. "Pampered, and every need provided for. Our stock works about sixteen seconds—that's two eight-second rides every six months. We do everything to minimize the danger to the animal and levy fines for riders who hurt one. After a few years of competition, the stock retire to a life of leisure. If only the folks from PETA could see the way we treat 'em, they wouldn't stand on the highway picketing our rodeos."

Obviously, she was not happy with the folks from the People for the Ethical Treatment of Animals.

23

The Greatest Show

ᴛᴇʀ ᴛʜᴇ ʀᴏᴅᴇᴏ's opening festivities, including the tradi-
ᴧal Quadrille performed by the youngest members of the Silver
ᴜrs, Clem asked everyone to stand, remove their hats, and cover
ir hearts for the singing of the national anthem and then to stay
nding for the invocation.

After the cheers for the anthem subsided, Clem delivered the
ening prayer in a made-for-radio voice rendered raspy after years
chain-smoking. His prayer that day, and one he became famous
, The Cowboy's Prayer, was more eloquent than one delivered by a
minary-trained pastor—and presented as only a true cowboy could:

*Our gracious and heavenly Father, we pause in the midst of this
festive occasion, mindful of the many blessings you have bestowed
upon us.*

*We ask that you be with us at this rodeo. As cowboys, Lord,
we don't ask for any special favors. We ask only that you will let
us compete in this arena as in the arena of life. We don't ask that
we never break a barrier, draw a chute-fighting horse, or draw a
steer that just won't lay. We don't even ask for all daylight runs.*

Alice also took us to the closest concession stand, where all the personnel were volunteers from the club. Dan Autrey and Hamp Sessions were flipping burgers and gave us a warm welcome. It was there I first met Jean Parten, who was not related to the Partins and would later become our office receptionist. She and Geech's wife, Connie, who had run the stand for decades, greeted us warmly and told us we were welcome to complimentary snacks during breaks in the action.

Alice and I left our boys at the concession stand to work with the crew while she took me to the announcer's platform. "Walt, this is Kathy Baker. She's one of Geech and Connie's five kids. Geech calls 'em his three kings and two queens."

Kathy blushed. "I'm too old to be called a kid, Alice. Anyway, Doc, good to meet you."

"She serves as the rodeo secretary," Alice explained. "She signs in all the competitors and dispenses, via check, their winnings. She's quite popular. Tell him about our competitors, Kathy."

"Some of the best in the business, including reigning and former world champions among them, make the February trip to Kissimmee for the Spurs. We rank among the PRCA's, that's the Professional Rodeo Cowboys Association, top fifty paying rodeos, and we're the largest rodeo east of the Mississippi River. Sometimes we'll have three to four days of slack."

Alice must have seen my confused look. "Slack is when excess entries in the events are scheduled for preliminary rounds of competition before the rodeo opens to the public."

Next to Kathy was a beautiful, hand-tooled saddle. "It's courtesy of the Saddle Rack," Kathy said. "Earl Evans, the owner, has donated a saddle to each rodeo since 1967. It's given to the winner of the All-Around Cowboy award. Earl also provides a pair of boots to the Silver Spurs Rodeo's Big Boss."

"Big Boss?" I inquired.

Kathy chuckled. "Our board of directors are all bosses. The chairman of the board is in charge of the rodeo and is called the

Big Boss. The vice chair is the Little Boss. (
Straw Boss, Round-Up Boss, and Old Boss

Alice pointed to a strikingly handsome, ta
haired man who was striding toward the st
announcer. He's from Chelsea, Oklahoma. H
ers 'cause he was born in Rogers County, Okla
nephew of Will Rogers," Alice crowed, as he
"He's by far our most popular announcer and
term state senator *and* US congressman from

Reaching the platform, he gave Alice a big
out his hand toward me. "Clem McSpadden,"
baritone voice and blushed as she continued
the PRCA Announcer of the Year and the Cc
Rodeo Man of the Year."

"As I always say, there's an amazing corre
career in rodeo announcing and politics," Cl
"There's way too much bull in each profession.

Clem and I became close friends over the ye

Alice and I returned to our seats in the first-
young Scotts sat on top of the protective steel fen
the arena. (Who knew that Alice's Scott would g
mous and very popular bullfighter—and a runner-
Champion.)

"Hey, Mr. Partin," Scott Ramsey called out,
fence to greet Geech as he walked up. "This is
Scott Larimore."

"Good to meet you, son. You got a resembla
here." He smiled at me, nodded, and said, "Mind i
with ya? Might be able to tell you a thing or two a
competed in quite a few of 'em back in the day."

"Are you kidding me? I'd be honored." I suspec
to experience the treat of a lifetime—having one o
mier horse and cattlemen serve as my personal tou
my first rodeo.[1]

*We only ask that you help us, Lord, to compete in life as hon-
est as the horses we ride and as clean and pure as the wind that
blows across this great land of ours. Help us, Lord, to live our
lives in such a manner that when we make that last inevitable
ride to the country up there, where the grass grows lush, green,
and stirrup high, and where the water runs cool, clear, and deep,
that you, as our last Judge, will tell us that our entry fees are paid.
Amen*[1]

It became my favorite Silver Spurs moment for many years.

The crowd settled into their seats and leaned forward as Clem
introduced the first event and competitor. Wild horses sprinted
from their pens underneath the stadium seats into the chutes where
stout metal gates clanged shut behind each, causing most to slam
the steel doors with their hooves and raising gasps from those
spectators new to rodeo. Every eye was riveted on the chutes, with
oohs and aahs elicited each time a horse reared up, trying to escape
its enclosure.

Clem commented, "Folks, the untamed horse or bull, unwilling
to bend their spirit to the whim of a cowboy, preferring to buck
him off and run free in the wild American frontier, is foundational
to rodeo, which is America's original pastime, one of the last blue-
collar sports in America. Modern rodeo began in 1869 when two
groups of cowboys from neighboring ranches met in Deer Trail,
Colorado. They wanted to settle an argument over who was the best
at performing everyday cowboy tasks. They decided on a competition in which the ranch hands would have to ride an unbroken
wild horse. We don't have a record of who won, but rodeo soon
spread across the west, events were added, and the rest is, as they
say, history. Now our broncs and bulls are all specially bred to buck
off anyone with the audacity to try to ride 'em.

"One of the stock contractor's men, each of whom knows their
horses well, places a strap snugly around the flank, while another
helper assists by cinching the bareback rigging down in the girth

area just behind the front legs. The rigging has a grip that resembles a suitcase handle atop the horse's withers."

"Those straps make the horse buck?" I asked Geech.

"They do, but not for the reason most think. The outside of the straps is made with leather while the inside is lined with sheepskin or neoprene. No sharp or cutting edges. It's impossible to damage any major organ with the straps. Even so, the rodeo judges inspect each horse to be sure all is safe."

"So they just buck on their own."

He laughed. "They give 'em a little help. One of the stock contractors pulls the flank strap snug at the very last second, just before the bronc takes his first leap into the arena. The stockman knows just how snug to pull the strap on each horse. It's not painful at all, but it bothers 'em, and they buck like crazy to get rid of that feeling. It's one reason the pickup men uncinch the strap as soon as the eight-second horn goes off. Don't want 'em getting used to it."

Clem's voice took over. "Why, then, when this unique horse wins a one-in-a-thousand chance to live his life untamed and bucks in a rodeo, do some consider it cruel?" he asked. "Today's modern saddle horses have been cultivated for centuries to be gentle and trainable. They breed bucking stock from the rare horse that comes along with a strong, natural desire to buck, an innate, undeniable inclination to buck wildly and wholeheartedly and not because they are in pain or because they are afraid. Horses that have that gift buck because that's their nature. And it creates a rare and dangerous competitor—one that bucks not only because it's born to but also because it loves to."

The two rodeo judges took up their positions, one on each side of the first gate that would be whipped open. They each would assign up to twenty-five points to the horse and up to twenty-five points to the cowboy. Their scores would be added together to result in a final score. Likely, it would take a score of ninety-four to ninety-six points to take home the champion saddle, $15,000 first-prize money, lifelong bragging rights, and the reputation of being a Silver Spurs Rodeo Champion, for which these men put life and limb at risk.

"I compare bareback riding to trying to control a giant jackhammer with one hand," Clem announced. "These cowboys may be our toughest."

"Tougher than bull riders?"

"Yep, because the bareback rider endures more abuse, suffers more injuries, and carries away more long-term damage than all other rodeo cowboys put together. Most of 'em have their orthopedic surgeon on speed dial."

Another horse reared in the chute, and his rider was violently thrown back. Two cowboys standing by the chute caught him.

"Man, he was lucky they were there!" I said.

"Weren't no luck, Doc," Geech explained. "We call them boys spotters. They stand on a catwalk behind the chutes for this specific reason. If they don't grab him, he could land under the horse's rear legs and be stomped pretty bad. Boys have been killed that way."

Clem continued, "As the bronc and cowboy come out of their chute, the rider must have both spurs touching the horse's shoulders until the horse's feet hit the ground after the initial leap from the chute. We call this *marking out*. If the cowboy does not do this, the judge will throw a red flag in the air, indicating the cowboy is disqualified. Then, as the bronc bucks, the rider pulls his knees up, rolling his spurs up the horse's shoulders. As the horse slams toward the ground, the cowboy straightens his legs, returning his spurs over the point of the horse's shoulders in anticipation of the next jump. The spurs are dull and do no damage to the horse's hide."

"Where do the competitors come from?" I asked Geech.

"From all over North America," he replied. "They drive or fly from most states, Canada, and Mexico. We even have some from Central America and Brazil. I like to say you have to be a cowboy before you can be a rodeo cowboy. Most of 'em, like me and my brothers, learn how to ride a horse before they can pedal a bike. But all of 'em are chasing eight-second dreams of fame. The average cowboy works a job all week long and competes in local or regional rodeos on weekends. Some are blessed with the God-given talent to rodeo full-time. They drive and live in what we call *rodeo motels*—the campers on their trucks or the ones they pull. Many of them will clock over 100,000 miles and rodeo as much as 200 to 250 days a year. We say they drive for a living and compete for fun—but all are pursuing their place in the Super Bowl of rodeo—the Wrangler National Finals Rodeo in Las Vegas. Very few make a lot of money—a few do, but only a few. But for every cowboy and cowgirl, rodeo is not just a weekend sport—it's everyday life."

Three men on horseback, with their ropes out, rode into the arena. These were the pickup men whose job it was, should the rider stay on, to ride up alongside the bucking bronc and pull the flank strap loose while the rider leaps off the horse and onto a pickup man's horse or does a running dismount on the ground. As one pickup man is doing this, the other two either herd the bronc to an exit gate or lasso it and lead it to the exit.

"Doc," Geech said, "most rodeos use only two pickup men. We'll use three or four because our arena can be used as a full football field. The stock is used to smaller arenas, so they get confused trying to find their exit gate." Pointing to a pickup man riding by, he commented, "They're all on Quarter Horses raised by me and my boys."

As a chute gate next to us clanged open, Geech exclaimed, "Get ready, Doc! The *real* Greatest Show on Earth is getting ready to start!"

The next year's rodeo found Barb and Kate working at the concession stand. The rodeo became a treasured family tradition for the Larimores.[2]

24

Professors

My time with Bill Judge was becoming increasingly valuable. He taught and modeled that our relationships with others were to involve sharing loving truth in discussion and service in deed. In short, by trying to follow Jesus's command to be salt and light.

Bill interpreted salt as meaning *speaking the truth in love* by having conversations that were missional and life-giving. He thought of light as meaning *living the truth* with competence by doing excellent work, with character by demonstrating integrity, and with compassion by displaying kindness.

Bill said God didn't call us as individuals to save the entire world but to influence the part of it into which he has placed us. "Mother Teresa," he said, "taught that not all of us can do great things, but we can all do small things with great love."[1]

My interactions with Robert opened my eyes to these truths. He was a big, burly man, a former NFL lineman and a new patient to our practice. During his first physical exam, I found an abnormal lump in his prostate. A biopsy showed early cancer. After considering his various options, which included a spectrum from watchful waiting to surgical removal, he decided, as was not unusual for most men in those days, to choose the latter.

Dr. Crespo was to perform the cancer surgery, a prostatectomy—the removal of his prostate. The day I admitted him, I went into the preoperative area to see him and his wife, as I would be assisting at surgery. We had a brief chat, and they assured me they were ready to proceed.

I heard my better side encourage me, *You're getting more comfortable with this prayer thing. And you're praying with most folks before surgery. Be salt and light today.*

Are you crazy? I heard my skeptical side inquire. *You don't know this man very well; you better not. You'll just upset him. And you don't want to increase his pulse, respirations, and blood pressure before surgery. Move on! How many times do I have to tell you, you're a doctor, NOT a pastor!*

I almost didn't say anything. *Salt and light,* the soft voice whispered. *Why not ask a simple question? He's a big boy. If he wants to refuse, he will. But don't pass on the opportunity to let him choose, not you.*

"Robert," I began, "is spirituality important to you?"

"Nope!" he exclaimed.

Told you! This IS a mistake! Now I was even more anxious. I felt palpitations but continued. "For me, it is. It's a part of my life and practice." His head nodded ever so slightly. "So I have a habit of offering a brief pre-op prayer for a safe surgery and rapid recovery for my patients. If you'd like that, I'd be happy to do so. If not, that's A-OK."

He paused a second, and I waited. I was sure he would not only say, "No!" but insert a swear word or two before it. I'm glad I was holding on to the gurney side rail with both hands because Robert stunned me by saying, "That'd be just fine."

Told you! murmured my better self, chuckling. As I quickly recovered from the astonishment and bowed my head for a brief prayer, I felt his large, calloused hand envelop and grip both of mine. When I finished, he did not relinquish his vice-like grasp. I looked up to see his lower lip quivering and a large tear flowing down his face. He sniffled and wiped his cheek with his free hand. I was quiet and observed a sacred moment in Robert's life. He composed himself after a minute and whispered, "You're not gonna tell anyone, are you?"

"What?" I asked. "That we prayed . . . or that you cried?"

"Nah," he replied as a wry smile crossed his face. "That we held hands."

"Better go scrub," I said, laughing.

Frank Crespo was at the scrub sink, operative cap and mask in place, soaping and scouring from his fingertips to above his elbows. As I walked up, he said, "I was standing outside pre-op when you prayed with Robert."

I cringed, uncertain what would follow. My critical side sneered, *Ridicule, criticism, scorn, derision—all are possible—and all are deserved.* I took the offensive. "It's something I've started to offer most of my pre-op patients."

Frank shrugged. "He's your patient. I guess you can do what you want." He rinsed his arms, holding them out with his hands up, elbows bent, water dripping to the floor as he gazed at me. His eyes seemed to soften. "I'm not a man of deep faith. Oh, I was religious as a kid. An altar boy—baptized and confirmed. The whole ball of wax. But I've gotten away from it all. Way away! Who knows? Maybe I'll go back someday."

It was my second shock of the morning. Midway through the surgery, during a moment's pause, I commented, "Frank, I appreciate you sharing with me a bit of your spiritual story. It's good to know where you're at in these things. Sometime let's talk a little more. I'll share my story with you."

He snorted and chortled. "Look, Walt. It was nice what you did for this fella. It was. But I don't think it's for me."

"Well, I'm glad you trusted me enough to tell me what you did."

Robert, Frank, and I would reminisce about that morning for some time, and I still think back on it fondly. Both are in heaven now, of that I'm sure. But that day marked the commencement of each man's spiritual journey. Robert gave his life to Christ two months later through the ministry and witness of several other folks. His spiritual growth was meteoric. God produced much fruit in him, his marriage, his family, and through them into our small town. He influenced many young men for Christ over the next two decades.

Frank's spiritual journey was rockier, which is understandable, as hard ground takes longer to cultivate—and some fruit takes longer to mature for the harvest. But I began to pray daily for him and enjoyed the time we spent together.

Robert and Frank were two of the many "professors" in learning to incorporate spirituality into conversations with patients, staff, and colleagues.

25

Friends

WE HAD SPENT far too many months searching for a church in which we could root and from which we could bear fruit in our daily lives. Finally, we visited a small congregation that was just starting up. The young pastor was winsome, charismatic, and a superb preacher. I was quite taken by him and loved his preaching; however, Barb had some doubts.

"What is it?" I would ask, but she never could put her finger on it.

"I sense there's something not right, but I'm just not sure what it is."

One weekend afternoon, I was mowing the front lawn when a car pulled up. A smiling, petite brunette popped out and walked over to me, saying, "Hi!" with a protracted, sweet Southern drawl.

"My name is Jennifer Adamson. My daddy is Bill Judge, and we've talked on the phone." I remembered calling each of Bill's girls and sons-in-law earlier in my mentoring.

She held out a round tin. "I've made some chocolate chip cookies for your family. I'd *love* to meet your wife. Is she here?" Barb came walking out, and as I finished mowing, the two of them chatted and were soon laughing.

After Jennifer left, Barb came over. "Do you know where she came from?"

"What do you mean?" I asked.

"*He* sent her over here to soften us up."

"*He* who?"

"She goes to *that* little church, and *that* pastor sent her over to entice us to return to *his* church. I know you admire him, but I'm suspicious. I don't trust him. He was too slick for my taste. But I like Jennifer. She could be my friend."

This was huge. Although Barb had many friends and acquaintances, she chose them very carefully. Her intuition about folks was remarkable. Nevertheless, despite Barb's initial misgivings about the pastor, we kept attending. The church membership multiplied. It was soon bursting at the seams, and they began looking for a larger building to accommodate the crowds. We quickly developed friendships with several young couples who attended the church and joined a small group with Jennifer and her husband, Jerry. The group was a superb support for us.

The Adamsons and their three girls lived close enough that we could walk to their home. Our kids and theirs played well together, even when Scott and their middle daughter, Darla, were bouncing on a trampoline, and Scott accidentally fell on Darla, breaking her ankle. Barb and Jennifer put almost five hundred miles on their "beach cruiser" bikes early in the mornings, riding to, from, and along the Toho lakefront and talking about and solving various family, church, and world problems.

In this small group, with these dear friends, we learned to apply biblical principles within the intimacy of relationships in community. We helped each other wrestle through questions we all faced about marriage and parenting and life. We studied how to walk with Christ more faithfully and to practice our biblical calling to love and serve others as we lived life together. We shared and listened to one another's dreams, adventures, issues, fears, mistakes, and problems. We learned how to intertwine our day-to-day lives and our spiritual development.

Although the fellowship, hospitality, accountability, discipleship, and Bible study we experienced together were precious, for Barb and me the most meaningful activity was learning to pray with and for each other. We had benefited by personal prayer, prayer as a couple, and prayer during worship services. But in the small group, we learned to pray in a new and more intimate way with other followers of Jesus. Our friends became not just our fellow travelers in our journey as young marrieds and parents but our teachers. We witnessed and experienced the biblical pattern of communal life in a spiritual community—and it turned out to be one of the best investments we could have made during our early years in our family and professional lives. When disasters descended, troubled waters threatened, or a storm swept over us, they were always there.

One of the couples in our small group had the same financial advisor we did, thus leading to an emergency visit one Saturday afternoon. They knocked on our door, unannounced, saying they needed to talk to us immediately. We could tell they were upset and invited them in. Before they were seated, the husband blurted out, "Have you heard about our retirement investment?"

Barb and I looked at each other and shook our heads. "Why?"

They sat down, holding hands. The woman began to cry, as he explained. "It's gone. All our money, all our retirement, our future is gone."

"What?!" I exclaimed.

"Turns out it's one of the largest Ponzi schemes in the history of Florida. That snake advisor of ours took the money from newer investors for his personal use and to pay off the older investors with so-called huge profits, although most of the money was on paper only. He found out the feds were on to him, so he took the money and ran. No one knows where he is. Our attorney is all over it but tells us he fears there's nothing we can do. I don't know about y'all, but we're ruined."

I was in shock. Absolute shock. If what they were saying was correct, we had just lost the equivalent of at least one year's income. Worse, we had borrowed a large sum of money from a local bank to get into the investment. But my immediate and overwhelming fear was not what was going to happen financially but what this would mean to our marriage.

Barb had been against the investment from the beginning, but I had decided to move forward with the deal on my own. It was an impulsive decision—not listening to my best friend, my wife, and my number one cheerleader, supporter, and advisor. I had not valued the gift of her intuition. I was now to learn from a painful personal experience what people far wiser and more observant than me understood—that almost all women have an amazingly accurate intuition. By not listening to and honoring Barb's unique gifting, the amount of money involved meant I potentially was driving us into bankruptcy.

Barb could have repeatedly said, "I told you so!" She could have harangued me to death with "Why didn't you listen to me?" She could have complained and nagged and driven me into depression or out of our home and marriage. But she did not.

"I trust the Lord," she softly told us all. "He does not cause or allow anything to cross our path that he won't use for our good and his glory."

"But," our friend's wife cried out, "this is devastating. This is terrible."

Barb walked over and sat by her. "It's not good news. It's awful news. But the Bible could not be clearer. It says, 'We know that in all things God works for the good of those who love him, who have been called according to his purpose.'[1] That's his promise, not mine. In all good things and in all bad things, if we love him and follow him, he'll lead the way, and he will turn it to good. We just have to trust him—his way—not our way."

"I wish I had your faith," the husband said softly.

"Me too," I muttered.

Barb had us hold hands, and she prayed for us all that God would provide wisdom and comfort, even during this difficult storm. We could have declared bankruptcy, but with prayer and counsel decided not to. As a result, we knew we were going to have to work hard to dig out of that debt. It was a painful process and required significant financial sacrifice and a lot of forced frugality. It was an agonizing lesson, indeed. But the road was more comfortable in that we walked it with our friends who loved, supported, encouraged, and prayed for us every step of the way.

26

Dunkin'

OUR CHURCH WAS ONE that emphasized baptism by immersion or, as some folks called it, *dunkin'*. It became an unexpectedly emotional issue for us. I had been baptized by "sprinkling" as an infant. Barb had been baptized by sprinkling when she was a teen as a requirement to join the church her family attended.

Once I chose to become a follower of Christ while in college, my mentors at the time encouraged me to be baptized by immersion. They said there was little doubt that the Bible commanded Christians to be baptized, and it was a symbol of Christ's saving work for the one being baptized and the public initiation, if you will, of a new believer into a community of believers, the church.

It had been a wonderful experience for me, and since Barb had never chosen to follow this sacrament as an adult, I began to encourage her—well, actually, I began to push her—to follow my example. After all, she had not been baptized since becoming a follower of Jesus as a young adult. Unfortunately, the pastor she was having difficulty tolerating began to push her at the same time. Both he and I were far too salty!

"Bill," I asked one morning at Joanie's, "how can I convince her?"

Bill smiled, thought a moment, and said, "Well, Walt, it's not your job, is it?"

I nodded. "Good. Then you'll do it?"

Bill laughed. "I most certainly will not! It's not my job, either!"

"Then whose job is it?"

Bill flipped open his Bible. "These are the words of Jesus toward the end of his life on earth. He was talking to his disciples and said, 'It is best for you that I go away because if I don't, the Advocate won't come. If I do go away, then I will send him to you. And when he comes, he will convict the world of its sin, and of God's righteousness.'[1] He's referring here to the Holy Spirit."

"I think I get what you're saying. Conviction is the Holy Spirit's job, not mine, correct?"

"God wants his followers to love folks. His inspired Word is for teaching, admonishing, correcting, and training his people. Teaching shows you the right path; admonition shows you when you've gotten off that path; correction shows you how to get back on the path; and training in righteousness shows you how to stay on the path."

I chuckled. "That's great, Bill. Where'd you get that?"

"It's straight from 2 Timothy 3:16. But to my main point, you're right. It's the Spirit's job to convict folks, not ours. So how about this? Why don't you and Barb and maybe the kids do a Bible study on the topic of baptism. See what he teaches you?"

It was a great idea, and for several weeks we did just that. One day when I got home from work, Barb and Kate were anxious to show me something they had learned.

"What surprised me, Walt," Barb explained, "is that the Greek word translated 'baptize' is used to describe the cleaning of jars or vases by immersing them in water."

"Or of ships that sink in water," Kate added.

"But what really got me, Walt, is that the word is used to describe the process of plunging cloth into a vat of dye. It literally means 'to dip' or to 'dip into dye.' And, of course, when it comes out, it has a new appearance, and its new color would now identify the cloth."

"It's not just 'cloth,' anymore," Kate said. "It's 'red cloth' or 'purple cloth.'"

Barb's eyes teared up. "It's a new identity, Walt. I see that now. To be immersed in his name is to become identified with him and his followers. I totally get it: as Christians, we are to proclaim our new life in Christ by being baptized publicly."

I sat down, stunned by what they were teaching me. My wife and daughter were serving as preceptors. "But what if someone is disabled and can't be immersed? Or if they're too old or crippled to get into the baptistry?"

"Immersion is important, I think," Barb said, "but public identification with Christ and his church is the critical issue. I'm convinced that *that* is the sacrament—the outward and visible sign of an inward, invisible change. The real deal is to identify as a follower of Jesus publicly. That's what's important."

Kate took Barb's hand. "We want to be baptized together."

"Wow!" was all I could whisper. "But, by our pastor?"

"That's the good news!" Barb exclaimed. "Jennifer says that in our church, a husband can baptize his wife and his children. Scott hasn't made a commitment to Christ yet, so I think he should wait. But Kate and I are ready. Will you do that for us?"

It's not your job! I could hear Bill say, and an internal voice whispered, *It's mine.* I couldn't speak, only nod in stunned silence, and then later experience the unmatched joy of baptizing my two sisters in Christ—my precious wife and daughter.

As the months went by, my now-baptized wife continued to express concern about our preacher. I, on the other hand, continued to be encouraged and educated by his teaching, preaching, and practices. And our kids adored him. When Kate's cat disappeared and never came home, Kate tearfully asked him, "Pastor, my kitty, Cinderella, is missing. If she died, will she be in heaven when I get there?"

I stood back and wondered how he'd answer. There was nothing in the Bible that I knew of about whether our beloved pets would or would not be in heaven, but how do you explain that to a heartbroken young girl?

He kneeled by her, took both of her hands in his, and said, "Kate, I can tell you with absolute certainty that if you *need* Cinderella to be with you for eternity, then your loving Father in heaven will provide her."

She hugged his neck as she cried. "Thank you, Pastor!" she whispered to what I perceived to be a sensitive, caring man.

Nevertheless, Barb's intuition continued to raise concerns for her, and we had long discussions about whether to stay or find a different church in which we all could be more comfortable. Our deliberations were rendered moot when the church suffered a painful split and eventually disbanded.

Once again, we were on the search for a new church, but within just a few months, our small group ended up at another church together. Our "family" was intact and, more importantly, Barb and I were on the same page. That was very good. Going to church together no longer resulted in Barb becoming anxious or concerned—and as Brother Bill observed, "Finally, y'all are as good as two peas in a pod and are grinning like possums."

27

Birthing

AFTER SOME TIME in practice together, John and I felt we had enough support in the hospital and community to begin applying more of the natural birthing philosophy and traditions I had learned from both lay and professional midwives in North Carolina. We were anxious to see if those Appalachian practices would work as well in Florida. To our delight, Dr. Gonzales, two female obstetricians, Sandi Lynch and several labor and delivery nurses, Jim Shanks, and Kevin Cole all agreed to support our efforts as long as we agreed to change things slowly—in other words, take baby steps.

As news leaked out, several of the older obstetricians voiced their displeasure and opposition. Mr. Shanks convinced them they would not have to change any of their practices. They let him know, in no uncertain terms, they would be watching us *very* carefully.

Our practice continued to grow, and we were gratified to receive more and more support from the community. As word spread, we attracted not only patients of all ages but increasing numbers of couples seeking a family physician to attend their births using these more natural techniques. This was an essential distinction to John and me. Highly technical birth professionals tended to see pregnancy as a disease that needed to be managed. We, however, saw it as part of God's divine design, and we were convinced that the more we taught, coached, and supported young couples, rather than try to intervene and manage their labor and delivery when not needed, the better the results for everyone involved.

Barb and Cleta, along with Judy and some of the hospital nurses, taught prenatal education classes. We strongly encouraged women to choose other women who had been through labor and delivery to accompany and support them during their birth process. Sometimes these women were volunteers—a sister, mother, best friend, pastor's wife—and sometimes they were professionally trained doulas.

If the father of the baby wanted to be involved, we wholeheartedly encouraged it. If he wanted to duck out from time to time, he was free to do so—and many did. It seemed to us that women who had been through labor were better able to care for other women during their birthing process. Either way, the studies showed—and our growing anecdotal experience confirmed—that the birthing outcomes and satisfaction were quite improved.

At the same time, Sandi and Jim invited John and me to be part of a team of several of the labor nurses and younger obstetricians who were open to more natural birthing. Jim brought in outside birthing experts to provide education and advice. He converted a couple of our labor rooms into birthing suites and began advertising the new services.

We stopped the use of routine IVs and continuous electronic monitoring, both of which kept women "harpooned" to a bed on their backs and seemed to slow down labor and make it more dysfunctional. We had women walk as late in labor as possible and deliver in whatever position was most comfortable for them, and we allowed them to have more than one support person.

I still smile when I remember learning, along with Sandi and the labor nurses, how to attend a birth whether a mother was in a knee-chest position, lying on her side, squatting, or even standing. It took both mental and some physical gymnastics, but it became our new normal in birthing. We no longer "delivered" babies; instead, we "attended" their births. It was strikingly popular with young families while earning the equally strong dismay of some of the older obstetricians.

Nevertheless, word of mouth spread, and we attracted young families from neighboring towns and even adjacent counties to our little hospital—which made Kevin Cole, Jim Shanks, and the board very happy. In Kissimmee, our support for what was then very unorthodox changes in birthing policy and practice grew. Of course, wherever there are positives, there are also potential potholes.

Some of the many reasons I loved practicing family medicine with John Hartman were the times each day we'd share puns and jokes, coffee breaks, Bible verses or information from a recent homily or sermon, fellowship, and life's ups and downs. We saw both gratifying and challenging cases together. It wasn't at all unusual for Judy or one of the other nurses to grab one of us and pull us over to the other's exam room to consult or pray with each other and a patient. One afternoon, I could see Judy was somber, and she had tears in her eyes.

"What is it?"

"Sad, sad case in Room 2. He needs you."

I knocked and entered. Barb was lying on the exam table, her eyes red and puffy. The ultrasound machine was at her side.

"I'm so sorry," John said softly.

"My all-day morning sickness disappeared this morning, just like with our last miscarriage, Walt," Barb whispered before blowing her nose. "The baby stopped moving."

She sat up, and I wrapped my arms around her as she cried.

"There's no heartbeat by fetoscope, and there's no sign of life on ultrasound." John wrapped his arms around us both and with a quivering voice, prayed over us and our baby.

John sent us home. He and the staff would care for my patients so that I could care for Barb. He was recommending twelve to twenty-four hours to see if Barb would go into spontaneous labor. If not, then he would offer us induction or a D&C to birth our baby. Induction was less costly but more painful and prolonged.

We went home. Jennifer and Jerry were kind to bring over dinner and then take the kids for a slumber party with their girls. Bill and Jane came by to pray with and over us. I took Bill aside and confessed, "Bill, I don't know what to do. I feel lost."

Bill reached into his back pocket, pulled out his well-worn Bible, and flipped to the Old Testament. "When King David and Bathsheba's baby boy died, this is what the Bible says he did: 'David comforted his wife, Bathsheba, and went in to her and lay with her.'¹ Just hold and hug, pray and cry. Just be together to comfort each other and let the Lord comfort you." He handed me his Bible and pointed. "Read this verse to me."

I read out loud, "King David said, 'While the child was still alive, I fasted and wept, for I said, "Who knows whether the Lord will be gracious to me, that the child may live?" But now he is dead. Why should I fast? Can I bring him back again? I shall go to him, but he will not return to me.'"²

"Walt, that's God's promise to you. That you will see this baby and the first one you lost once again. And he has another promise for you that as a physician you need to know." He took his Bible back and turned to the New Testament. After flipping a few pages, he said, "Here it is. Listen carefully: 'Blessed be the God and Father of our Lord Jesus Christ, the Father of mercies and God of all comfort, who comforts us in all our affliction.'³ The first promise is that he will comfort you two, and Kate and Scott also when you tell them. But, here's the second promise—a reason for our suffering—he 'comforts us in all our affliction, so that we may be able to comfort those who are in any affliction, with the comfort with which we ourselves are comforted by God.'⁴ He will redeem this, Walt. He will."

That night we didn't sleep much—we just held each other, cried, and prayed. We read Scripture to each other, and several times we softly sang:

> When peace, like a river, attendeth my way,
> When sorrows like sea billows roll;
> Whatever my lot, Thou hast taught me to say,
> It is well, it is well with my soul.[5]

A few months later, Barb and I were enjoying a cup of coffee on our back porch. We were quiet and enjoying listening to the birds chirping in the trees. The aroma of the coffee and the fresh scents of spring wafted over and around us. Barb was looking over the yard, and I was overcome with how beautiful she was—not just on the outside but in her spirit. Our grief over our loss had slowly dissipated, and our times of laughter and joy were increasing.

She turned to look at me. "What are you staring at?" she said, smiling.

"The most beautiful woman I know."

"That's sweet. But that woman has an idea to share with you."

"I'm ready."

"What would you think about a new ministry in your office?"

"Such as?"

"A lay minister ministry."

"What's that?" I asked.

She looked back over our yard as her eyes filled tears. "I thought we could minister to other couples who have lost a baby. Then, whenever the practice has a couple who loses a child before birth, if the couple wants, we could be called to come minister to them—be with them, listen to them, pray with them. What do you think?"

I nodded. "Great idea, babe. It will allow us to comfort with the comfort with which we have received." I put my cup down, scooted over, and hugged this amazing woman.

It was the birth of a new ministry for us and the practice, which allowed us to match patients experiencing a medical or emotional crisis with patients of ours who had struggled with, survived, and even eventually thrived because of the same issues. It grew over the years to include cancer survivors—for example, Robert and his wife ministered to couples going through prostate cancer—and others with a wide variety of diseases and disorders. Our practice no longer had health professionals and lay ministers who just went to church. We were a practice of caring Christians who became the church every day.

28

A Curious Case

ONE OF JOHN'S AND MY most curious and challenging cases was a very alternative-medicine-oriented woman from a neighboring county who fixated to the extreme on natural health approaches. She was a true zealot about these things. We had to navigate her and her family's health care with a great deal of careful negotiation.

When Hadlee wanted her six-year-old son to be a birth doula instead of her husband during the delivery of their second child, Judy helped steer the unusual request through Sandi Lynch and the birthing suite administrators.

Thankfully, Hadlee had a professional doula and a sister who cared for her son during the birth process. When she wanted to take the child's placenta home to prepare placenta-based lasagna, we even rolled with that.

Her husband, a cowboy on a large ranch, dolefully commented, "Well, them cows lick their calves clean and gobble down their afterbirth, so the smell don't attract predators. Seems to be the nature of things."

I wanted to remind him that we had never had a beast of prey attack a baby at our hospital but held my tongue. I was just glad Hadlee didn't want to tongue-bathe her baby!

To our surprise, Sandi shared with us reports from around the country of others who provided alternative forms of maternity care, allowing and even encouraging such things. We also found a book of recipes for placenta-based drinks and meals. Nevertheless, it seemed that there were far more folks to whom *placentophagy* (placenta eating) was stomach-churning, including us, than the rare aficionados of *placenta parmigiana* or *afterbirth Alfredo.* To John and me, it was just plain weird.

However, what was beyond the pale, at least for me, was to walk into the exam room for a well-child visit and find Hadlee breastfeeding both her two-week-old son *and* her six-year-old son together—one on each breast. Imagine my shock! I had never heard of much less seen such a thing. I was quite taken aback, but doctors often see appalling things and are trained and accustomed to keeping a calm demeanor and poker face.

"Hadlee," I said, taking my seat, "I'm surprised you're still breastfeeding your older son." She unlatched both children, buttoned her blouse, and replied, "Oh, not exclusively. Only first thing in the morning, when he gets home from school, and at bedtime. I lay down with him and read him a story as he breastfeeds himself to sleep. Especially when daddy's out on the range."

I took a deep breath, concerned about some deep-seated psychopathology. I needed to talk to colleagues and gain some education about this before discussing it with Hadlee, which I knew I could do at her six-week postpartum visit or the newborn's two-month well-child visit.

John was as stunned as I was. But the more folks we talked to and the more we read, the more astounded we became. We found experts for and against what they called *long-term* or *extended breastfeeding.* Those for it argued that it was a common practice for "lots and lots and lots of people" in the United States and many other Western countries. They claimed it gave the child and mother emotional and physical benefits and was not as rare or as unusual as most of our colleagues thought. But these experts advised mothers to be quiet, even secretive, about the practice or face the risk of being accused of sexual abuse and having their child removed by child protective services and losing them in custody battles. There were cases in which both had happened.

However, we found far more professionals opposed to extended breastfeeding—especially after age three or four. These authorities believed it wasn't necessary, nurturing, or normal. They said there were no proven benefits to the mother or for the child—but there were clear downsides. For example, they believed it could lead to the child being ridiculed and, even worse, could cause the child to become abnormally dependent on the mother. In Hadlee's case, we suspected that this mother was unusually, maybe even pathologically, dependent on her son.

In our practice, we encouraged exclusive breastfeeding until the child was six to twelve months old—preferably the latter. We recommended continued breastfeeding when desired until age two. A number of mothers who had successfully breastfed their babies joined our growing breastfeeding support team.

But breastfeeding to age six? To our surprise, we learned the American Academy of Pediatrics had declared that breastfeeding should continue "for one year or longer as mutually desired by mother and infant."[1] But we wondered whether "mutual desire" beyond age two or three was healthy or harmful. To us, at least in this case, the practice was of great concern—and, it turned out, was equally disturbing to her husband. For him, it was the tipping point of a giant iceberg of suppressed problems and emotions swirling around his growing relationship difficulties with Hadlee.

I recommended they see a Christian psychologist, and during therapy, the skilled counselor uncovered several significant personality and emotional disorders in Hadlee's soul. To the couple's credit, they attempted to deal with each one. Fortunately, the breastfeeding of the older child stopped, but sadly, the marriage shattered. Hadlee and her children moved away, and we never heard from them again.

PART FIVE

29

The Littlest Cowboy

ONE SATURDAY MORNING on a rodeo weekend, our ever-rambunctious and hardheaded Scott woke before dawn and donned his new cowboy outfit—well, at least part of it. He wore the hat and boots but left his new cowboy shirt and Wrangler jeans on his bed to wear his more-comfortable T-shirt and shorts. He and a partner cowpoke, Cameron, were riding bikes in the neighborhood when I arrived home from making rounds at the hospital. I herded them into the kitchen where Kate was reading and began our tradition of fixing French toast together while Barb enjoyed a well-earned slumber.

This wasn't just any run-of-the-mill, plain-ole-average French toast. It was *pain perdu*. For those not in the know about South Louisiana traditions, *pain perdu*, pronounced *pan pear-dew*, is the *original* French toast. It has a crisp, buttery exterior and a delicious custardy interior. Unlike its inferior American cousin, which is made with plain, ordinary sandwich bread, we made *pain perdu* with thick, crusty French bread. When I couldn't get French bread, I'd substitute challah bread. But, either way, we'd wait until it began to get a bit stale, or *lost*, as a New Orleanian would say.

175

Even stale French bread, which is still tastier than regular bread, was perfect for "lost bread," or in French, *pain perdu*.

The kids pulled chairs up to the counter. As the griddle was heating, we'd whisk up a custardy mixture of eggs, all-purpose flour, whole milk, heavy cream, unsalted butter, granulated cane sugar, vanilla, cinnamon, and nutmeg. We'd allow the one- to one-and-a-half-inch bread slices time to soak up the creamy liquid.

The aromas floating around the kitchen were delectable, and the *pain perdu* was, as always, delicious. The kids would slather butter, syrup, and sometimes strawberries on top of their fried bread. I'd continue cooking until I had a large pile prepared. Any uneaten slices could be frozen. We could also pop individual pieces into the toaster oven for a quick and tasty, if not entirely healthy, breakfast on school mornings.

While I was cleaning up and putting on a pot of coffee for Barb and me to enjoy, Kate went back to her book, and the boys headed out to herd up more imaginary cattle and ride the range, looking for bandits and desperados to banish. Our neighborhood was extremely safe as a result.

While Barb and I sipped our coffee and talked about our plans for the day, the door from our garage to the kitchen flew open. Edna Thacker rushed in and, with no greeting or howdy-do, exclaimed, "*Your* boy is in trouble. You need to come get him. Now!"

She rushed back out, we looked at each other in dread, and without a word followed in a panic. Had he fallen off a bike? Been hit by a car? Bitten by a snake?

We ran behind Edna and around her house to the front yard. She pointed up to her rooftop, and to our horror, there was Scott, running up and down the ridge of her steeply pitched roof. He was riding a stick horse and whooping at the top of his lungs. He would stop every few steps to put the stick, now an imaginary rifle, to his shoulder to aim at Cameron, who was running from bush to bush and returning fire from his stick rifle.

Barb screamed, "Scott!"

He couldn't hear her over the gunfire.

"How'd he get up there?" I asked Edna.

"Probably on the side of the house. There's a concrete block wall next to the house."

I ran around the house, found the wall, made it to the roof, and carefully walked up the steep pitch. *How'd the boy do this in cowboy boots?* was all I could think.

Once I approached the ridgeline, Scott saw me.

"Hey, Dad!"

"Scott! Come over here. Now!"

I imagine he heard the concern in my voice because he immediately obeyed. I took his hand, and we began carefully walking down. Then it happened. Scott slipped and began to stumble forward. Had I not had his hand and been leaning backward, we would have tumbled head over heels and fallen a good twelve to fourteen feet to the ground. Fractured bones, a broken neck, concussion, and traumatic brain injury were diagnoses that rushed through my mind.

Once we safely dismounted the roof, Barb sternly took Scott's hand and marched him home. I turned to face what I imagined would be the not-too-subtle Cajun wrath of my neighbor. I was sure a lecture or sermon on poor parenting was about to rain down, but as Barb and Scott disappeared from view, a luminous smile and a deep chuckle erupted.

"My goodness!" was all she could mutter as she began to laugh. "How Scotty reminds me of my boys. Clarence and Rusty were getting in trouble all the time. I'm just thankful for neighbors who helped keep an eye on them. I learned you have to work hard to keep little boys out of trouble, but you can't keep them out of your heart. After all, they're the raw material the good Lord uses to make men, don't you think?"

"I do, Edna. And I'm thankful for your watchful eyes. That could have turned out bad."

"It wasn't my eyes, Walt. I was in my kitchen and heard a clomping sound on my roof. For the life of me, I couldn't imagine what it was. I went outside, and what to my wondering eyes should appear—your son. He wouldn't listen to me, so that's when I ran to get you. Like my husband, Russell, says, 'With little boys, you always know where you stand. And it's right in the path of an oncoming tornado!' But I still love the boys I raised, even though they're now men. I tell Russell, 'They've left happy smudges and fingerprints all over my heart!'"

Walking through the door from the garage to our kitchen, I found Barb sitting at our kitchen table and looking out at the backyard.

"Where's Scott?"

"I sent him to his room. He's in time-out."

"For how long?"

She shrugged. "Maybe until high school."

I laughed, poured myself a cup of coffee, and sat down. "You gotta admit, it *was* pretty funny."

She turned, and I could see her tear-stained cheeks. "Nothing funny about it, Walt. He could have been seriously hurt or have died. I've already lost two children before I could even hold them in my arms. I can't imagine losing one in childhood." She buried her face in her hands.

Pulling my chair close, I held her tight. "I'm sorry."

"I've been in enough hospitals—two miscarriages, Kate's surgeries and never-ending therapy sessions, your incapacitating migraines and recurrent collapsed lungs in medical school and residency. If I don't see another emergency room, that's too soon for me!"

I had no idea this event would affect her so profoundly. "I'll go talk to him."

"No! Don't!"

"Why not?"

"Let's just leave him in there."

"How long?" I asked.

178

"Until he's grown up." She sniffled and smiled at herself. "Can't we do that?"

I smiled and shook my head. "No, honey. Our job is to love him like he is and do the best we can."

Barb nodded. "I guess we need to do all that's possible to be good parents and let God deal with the impossible."

"That *is* his job," I said, hugging her close. "And that's my prayer."

30

One Tough Cowboy

GEECH, ALICE, AND I settled into our chairs behind the arena fence just outside the first-aid room for the first day of another Silver Spurs Rodeo. During my first several rodeos, we were fortunate to have had no significant injuries. The more I communicated with other rodeo doctors around the county, the more I realized how unusual my experience was. That was to change today.

The cowboy astride the first bareback bronc was holding on for dear life, grasping the small leather handhold just behind the bronc's shoulders with his right hand. The large crowd gasped as the horse exploded out of the chute and into the air, leaping until his hooves were three to four feet off the dampened loam of the stadium floor.

The bareback rider threw himself backward until his backbone collided with that of his steed, his left arm held high beside his Stetson hat. Upon landing, the horse flung himself into a spinning helicopter move. He was doing anything and everything he could to shorten either the ride or the life of the enemy who was running spurs up and down his shoulders. The stallion believed he was being bitten by something that needed to be bucked off as soon as possible.

The horse's enlarged eyes looked like small white saucers as he threw his head up and down. The veteran cowboy knew he needed to stay on for eight seconds with perfect form, all the while spurring his horse to more brutal bucks, twists, and jumps as two expert PRCA rodeo judges stayed as close as possible, scrutinizing for any mistakes.

With the bronc's third violent leap into the air, the cowboy lost his grip and flew straight up. I'm sure my eyes widened as he kept going up, his legs looking as if he were riding an invisible bike and his arms rotating like windmills to stay upright and land, hopefully, on his feet. His boots were at least ten feet off the rodeo floor when the cowboy began to fall.

Knowing the arena dirt was dampened before each event to be firm enough for the animals to get traction but sufficiently soft for the cowboys to land on without getting hurt, I was optimistic this would turn out all right. It relieved me to see him land first on his left leg and then an instant later on his right. But my delusion that he would be safe was shattered as I watched his left leg buckle in horror. From a distance, it appeared the shin bent out ninety degrees at or just below the knee. An audible pop from his leg and a grunt from his throat coincided and echoed around the stadium as spectators groaned and jumped to their feet. The man collapsed like a ragdoll, and his head slammed into the ground. He lay unconscious and didn't move.

As the judges raced to him, I saw the EMTs grab a bodyboard and sprint to the cowboy's aid.

"I think that boy's hurt bad," Geech whispered. "What 'cha think? Broke a bone or two in his leg? Tib-fib?"

"Could be," I said, nodding and trying to hide the nausea I was fighting after seeing the gruesome injury. The pickup men had uncinched and roped the bucking horse to prevent him from running back over the cowboy while the EMTs straightened the leg enough to put on a splint. The arena was whisper quiet as Clem explained the rescue process to the crowd and then led a brief prayer for the cowboy's recovery.

"My guess," I said, "is that he's likely blown out his knee. May have ruptured one or two ligaments, the medial collateral and ACL both, I suspect, and perhaps his meniscus too."

The EMTs placed the now conscious cowboy on the bodyboard. He pushed his upper body up on one elbow and tipped his hat to the crowd, which collectively sighed in relief and applauded.

Alice threw open the gate as the EMTs brought the man into the first-aid room and laid him on a bed. We all followed them into the room.

The cowboy looked at Geech. "Good to see you, Mr. Partin."

"You too," Geech responded.

"Most cowboys, especially those from Florida, know him. He's a hero to most of 'em," whispered Alice.

I introduced myself and asked some basic questions. He had been in good health, had no chronic diseases, and was taking no medications. "Nothin' 'sides the occasional ibuprofen for cowboy aches," he said, smiling.

I asked the EMTs to take off the splint. As one was doing so, the cowboy pushed his upper body up, resting on his elbows to watch the proceedings. I asked the other EMT, "Knee?"

He shook his head. "Nope."

Before I could question him further, the splint was off. I could see the man's lower leg angulated about ten to fifteen degrees halfway between the knee and the ankle.

"Looks like a fracture of your tibia and fibula, the two lower leg bones," I explained.

The cowboy smiled as he looked up at me. "No kidding, Tonto."

"No kidding." I knelt next to him and saw there was no blood on his jeans over the fracture site. It was a good sign. The fracture was closed, meaning the bone ends were not sticking through the skin, which would have skyrocketed his risk of infection. Quickly palpating the area, it felt like the skin was intact.

"I need to take your boot off," I told him. "It'll hurt like the dickens."

"Do what 'cha gotta do, Doc."

I knew it would be difficult to cut the boot off, but I also knew that if I pulled the boot off in such a way as to align the ankle and knee, I could both reduce the fracture and diminish the pain he must have, despite his looking calm and collected.

"Lean back; I've got a bite block." Hopefully, it would help suppress the scream that would surely come when I pulled off the boot. The broken bone edges were saturated with angry nerve endings and would send a horrible electric shock up his body. "When I take off your boot, I'll also be trying to reduce the fractures—to line the bones up best I can. It'll only take a few seconds, but you will feel like you've been shot or stabbed. It'll hurt bad."

"I'll be fine, Doc," he said matter-of-factly. "Don't need no bite block."

"I bet he won't even whimper," Alice said. She smiled at him. "These guys are pretty dern tough. Have an amazing pain threshold."

I positioned myself at the end of the bed, thinking, *They are not aware of the pain he will go through here in a second.* But I knew I could accomplish what I needed to in only a few seconds. A torturous instant, to be sure, but hopefully a brief one.

It turned out that I was the one who did not understand. I gently lifted the broken leg, one hand behind the boot heel, the other over the instep. I stabilized one of my boots against the end of the bed and said, "You ready?"

He nodded, and in one quick motion, I pulled the boot as hard as I could to both remove the boot and at the same time distract the bone ends so that when I let off the pressure, hopefully, the boot would be off and the bony alignment would be reasonable. The man's eyes widened as he collapsed on the bed. He grimaced but made no sound at all. To my great relief, I felt the large bone, the tibia, snap into place. I kept the distracting pressure and called for Alice.

She stepped over. "Hold his lower leg in position with both of your hands." I finished pulling off the boot, and Alice lay his leg on the bed. I reached under his jeans and felt along the shin and fibula. To my pleasant surprise, they were smooth at the fracture site. No step off at all. "Success!" I exclaimed. "Feels almost perfect."

The cowboy was pale, and beads of sweat had broken out on his brow. But with pursed lips, he tried to smile.

"I need to cut your jeans. That okay?"

He looked unsure, maybe even panicked a bit.

Alice reassured him, "I'll cut along the seam. It'll be easy to stitch up. You'll never notice the difference."

I examined the disrobed leg. His sensation was intact everywhere I touched. His foot arteries were pulsating normally. I squeezed his big toe, and upon letting go, the nail bed flushed, indicating good blood flow. "I'm happy with the reduction—the way I've gotten the ends of the broken bone back in place," I said to all observers. "The circulation to your foot is normal, and I don't think you have any nerve or blood vessel damage. Also, you're lucky the bone ends didn't come through the skin. A closed fracture heals much faster than an open one."

"I appreciate it, Doc."

"I'll need the EMTs here to put the splint on, so they can transport you over to the hospital."

"Won't be necessary," he said. "I'll be all right."

"Nope," I countered, "I need to ship you over there. It won't take long. You'll be back in a jiffy."

"Ain't going!"

"Why not?"

"Why? Why go through the expense?"

"Well, first, we need to do an X-ray."

A smile crossed his face, and he looked at me as if to say, *duh*, but politely offered, "Doc, it's broke." I could hear Geech chuckling behind me.

I felt my cheeks flush. "I know. But I want to be sure the reduction is adequate."

He glanced at his leg and observed, "It's straight enough for me, Doc. Once it mends, it'll be just fine."

"Even so," I protested, "the EMTs need to take you there so I can get you casted up and on some crutches. You shouldn't bear weight on that leg until checked by an orthopedic doctor."

A somber look spread across his face. "Won't need either."

"Why not?" I asked incredulously.

The door to the first-aid room opened and in walked two cowboys. To my amazement, one had a pair of crutches, and the other had two halves of a fiberglass leg and foot cast. Alice and Geech began to chuckle, as did the cowboy.

"Doc, I done broke this leg 'bout two weeks ago. Got it reduced and casted. A pal of mine, a rodeo doctor, bivalved my cast with a cast saw. I take it off to ride and tape it on when I'm done. Had that fool horse not bucked me so high, I'd have just landed on my good leg, backside, or back, and a pickup man would have taken me to the paddock. Anyway, I'm gonna cast up and head to the airport. We're catching a plane this evening for Ruston, Louisiana. I gotta ride there tomorrow."

I'm sure you could have knocked me over with a feather. After the cowboys left, Alice assured me that this was typical behavior for these amazing men. "Their pain threshold is through the roof, exceeded only by their pride. In fact, I'm kinda surprised they even let the boys bring him in here."

"Do you ever worry about being sued for malpractice?"

Her eyes widened. "You kidding me? Wouldn't happen. Not with this stock. They're good folk."

Geech chuckled. "You can tell how good a man and a watermelon are when they get thumped. And that man's a good 'un. Like an old Timex watch. Takes a lickin' and keeps on tickin'." His smile spread from ear to ear.

"Wow," was all I could say.

"Welcome to Rodeo 101," Geech added, laughing. "But you're off to a good start, son. Sometimes you get, and sometimes you get got. You got got good, but that ole boy'll spread some good talk about 'cha. That'll be good for you and for the Spurs. Well done."

For three to five days, twice a year, Alice and I had ringside seats, alongside a local cowboy and rodeo hero, to watch our Scotts grow into young men at an American spectacle as pure as the old Wild West itself. Barb and I were never invited to join the Silver Spurs Riding Club, I suspect because no one knew one of our grandpaps "real good." But they were sure a significant influence on me and my family.

31

Stinging

From time to time, I'd visit Jim and Cynthia Sabetto at their orchid business near our home on weekends, enjoying their massive collection and extensive greenhouses. Through the years, Barb and I purchased their flowering beauties as gifts or to grow ourselves. The climate in Central Florida was ideal for many types of orchids, and these generally forgiving plants made us look like we had green thumbs!

The fragrance they released when flowering was unique and delightful. Jimmy told us, "That fragrance plays a critical role in their survival. Just as folks wear perfume or cologne to attract others, orchids spice up their life to attract pollinators—bees, butterflies, hummingbirds, moths, even beetles and wasps. They pick up the sticky pollen as they feed and transfer it to other flowers."

He had given me a tour when I first arrived—like a father proud to show off his children. "Smell these *Dendrobium*." One smelled like raspberry and another like strawberry. "This *Lycaste* has the aroma of cinnamon. In fact, its species name is *aromatica*. Over here is a *Maxillaria* that smells like coconut, and next to it is the chocolate and vanilla perfume of an *Oncidium*, sometimes called *dancing ladies.*" He picked up his pace. "We need to hurry. I have two you *have* to smell before they fade."

As we walked, he explained, "Most orchids smell best when the light is brightest in the early hours of the day. This matches the activity of the pollinators that are more active in the early hours. Others are more fragrant in the afternoon and still others at dusk when nocturnal pollinators, like moths, come out." We arrived at two gorgeously blooming orchids. "What's this *Phalaenopsis* smell like to you?"

One sniff, and I knew. "Rose."

Jimmy smiled and moved to the next one. "Everyone loves your bubble gum, so I saved the best for last. It's a *Vanda coerulescens.* Vandas are my favorite orchid. Smell this one!"

There was no mistaking it. "Grape bubble gum!"

My love affair with orchids began in earnest. In exchange for helping repot orchids during Saturday morning visits, Jim and Cynthia let me take the sicker plants they were planning to throw away. To their and my surprise, some survived. Within a few years, I had a growing collection of some spectacular orchids.

Cultivating orchids is like raising children. They take a lot of patience, a suitable growing environment, excellent nutrients, and loving training. Then they can bloom in such a way that their appearance and fragrance will be attractive and sweet for all to admire.

One Saturday, I was working in the small fiberglass paneled and roofed greenhouse Jimmy had helped me construct in our side yard. I heard horrifying screams, followed by loud crying. A voice was yelling, "Mama! Mama!" It was from Scott.

I sprinted to the front yard, where Barb joined me. We saw Scott, Cameron, and another of their neighborhood friends, Brad, clinging to each other, half limping, half running toward us, wailing in pain.

We ran to them. "What happened?"

"We got stung by yellowjackets!" Scott cried.

I could see the whelps beginning to rise on the boys' arms and legs. Dan Autrey's near-fatal reaction to yellowjackets immediately came to mind. Fortunately, the boys' faces seemed clear. Their pulses and respiratory rates were elevated as expected due to their fright, but fortunately, they were not wheezing or in any respiratory distress.

"Boys, no sign of dangerous allergic reaction. You'll be okay." I turned to Barb. "Could you run to the house and pull out the gel packs from the freezer?"

They continued to cling to each other, whimpering.

"Let's go to the house. We'll put on some first-aid cream and then ice packs. With that and some antihistamine and ibuprofen in your system, you'll feel better in no time." As we were treating them at our kitchen table, Russell and Edna burst through the back door.

"Are they okay?" Edna asked, rushing over to inspect each of them as only a trained nurse and mother can.

I assured her they were fine, but being the excellently trained nurse she was, she needed to convince herself.

"Were you boys in my side yard?" Russell asked sternly.

They looked at each other and nodded. "Are we in trouble *again*, Judge?" Cameron asked.

Russell knelt. "No, no. Not at all. It's just I need to find 'em. Did you run into a nest hanging from a branch?"

"No, sir," Brad answered, his lips still trembling. "We were just exploring the woods between your home and mine. Scott stepped into a hole or something. He was up to his hip and couldn't get out. He started screaming. Cameron and I were trying to pull him out when we were all attacked by the yellowjackets. We pulled on Scott as hard as we could. When we finally got him out, we ran like crazy, trying to swat them off, but they chased us."

"That's the truth, Judge," Scott added. "I was stuck. If they hadn't dragged me out, I would have died!"

189

Judge Thacker's face lost all color. He took a deep breath and let it out as he thought. "Walt, if you think the boys will be okay, let's go look. I suspect I know what happened."

We walked across the street, around his house, and to the edge of the fifty- to sixty-foot-wide overgrown strip between his home and the neighbor's. There was thick underbrush carpeting the ground below a tall tree canopy. We slowly walked to the edge of the thicket. The air was moist and cool. We were downwind, and the musty aroma encircled us as a gentle breeze blew from the lake. He indicated I should stand behind him as he stopped and gazed for a moment. Over his shoulder, he whispered, "Come up. *Very* slowly."

When I was beside him, he pointed. "See that slight depression in the ground?"

It took a few seconds before I could discern it. "I do."

"Looks to be the size of a grave, doesn't it?"

In fact, he was right. "Maybe two to three feet wide, five or six feet long." I felt my eyes widen. "You don't think?"

"No, it's not a grave. But if it is what I expect it is, it could very well have been your son's."

I looked at his face and could see he was not kidding. Looking back at the depression, I could now see the hole made by Scott's leg and saw yellowjackets coming and going through it and several other smaller holes. "The nest is in the ground?"

He nodded. "Let's slowly back up to a safe distance."

Once we were well away from the nest, Russell explained, "Yellow-jackets usually make their nests in trees. But as is the case here, they'll also nest in holes dug by rodents and moles. These ground nests are the worst because they offer protection against easy removal and are much harder to see. Therefore, they're much more dangerous."

"How so?" I asked.

"These little buggers are known for their bad tempers. And they are extremely protective of their nest. You can agitate them just by walking by—mowing the lawn or watering flowers near them. Ground vibration, even loud laughter or shouting nearby, can cause yellowjackets to go on the attack in an instant to protect their nest. There is no insect in our area more aggressive than a yellowjacket. But if you poke or step on their nest, well, that'll cause the most rapid and violent reaction of all. As the boys learned, they can swarm mighty fast. I've seen them fly in circular patterns like a tornado and head toward flesh like metal shavings to a magnet. What's worse is that their stinger can stab the skin several times in rapid succession."

"I thought the stinger came out after one sting," I said.

"That's true for bees. But yellowjackets are in the wasp family—and the females can sting multiple times without losing their stinger. Folks say it feels like a hot poker on the skin."

"I bet the boys would agree."

"For most, the stings just hurt like the dickens. For others, the venom is toxic and causes a severe reaction requiring emergency care. Sorta like when you took care of Dan Autrey when that happened to him up in North Carolina."

"He could have died."

"Yep. I've seen 'em even kill a calf."

"Really?"

"When I was a kid, some friends and I were riding in a pasture. We came across a yellowjacket nest in the ground with a small calf stuck in it up to its tummy. The colony had killed it and were slowly eating the carcass."

"Can we drown them?" I asked.

Russell shook his head. "Filling a nest hole with water will only infuriate them. Wasp spray or insecticide is not helpful for a nest this big. That'll only kill the ones at the top and leave the ones at the bottom to crawl over the poisoned bodies even madder than before."

"Do we call someone? A professional?" I asked.

Russell shook his head. "Nope. I'll show you how ranchers take care of this. But it won't be until tomorrow morning. We'll come back when it's cool, and they are still asleep."

At dawn, Scott and I met Cameron, Brad, and Russell at the Thackers'. Russell had already positioned two fire extinguishers and water hoses with nozzles about twenty feet from the nest. He had a bucket and two sticks with a linen ball at the end of each one. From a container labeled KEROSENE, he poured a quart or so of the fuel into a bucket and soaked the linen with the fuel.

"Here's the plan," Russell explained. "You boys all stay well away. Once Doc and I start, they will swarm like crazy."

The boys began to back up.

"Walt, I'll light the torches for you to carry, and I'll carry the bucket of kerosene. Then we'll cautiously approach the nest. On the count of three, I'll toss the kerosene on the nest and grab one of the torches. We'll toss them on the nest and walk away slowly. Do *not* run. That only attracts them to you. Understand?"

"Won't this cause an explosion?" I asked.

"No," answered Russell. "The leaves and nest material will serve as a wick. The kerosene will light gradually, but then it'll burn for quite a while."

"Well," I said, "sounds like a plan. But how about we ask the Lord for safety?" I said a quick prayer, and we put Russell's plan into action.

After we lit the torches, we crept to within three feet of the nest. "One, two, three," Russell counted out. At the count of three, he slung the liquid across the den and grabbed a torch. We both threw ours on the nest and gently backed away.

To my surprise, no yellowjackets were swarming. "Did we catch them sleeping?" I asked.

"It's cool, so they are likely deep in the nest. But listen!"

We heard a cacophony of angry buzzing coming from the ground, even from a distance of fifty to sixty feet. We all watched with widening eyes as the flame built. The hoses and fire extinguishers were ready, but only the nest burned. It took quite a while for it to burn out, but by then, we could see no yellowjackets. The depression in the ground was now about two feet deep.

"It was a huge nest!" was all I could say. I was astounded.

"Looks like we got them all," Russell said. "But let's not take a chance. Because of the possibility of a deeper colony, let's use up the last of the kerosene just to be sure."

After the second burn, the nest hole was three feet deep. Russell declared the threat nullified, and we all marched to our kitchen for congratulatory sandwiches, cookies, and milk.

Cameron exclaimed, "Mrs. Barb, you make the best peanut butter and jelly sandwiches in the world. I could eat these sandwiches every day. I'm not sure what you do to them, but they are my favorite."

Barb leaned over to Russell and whispered, "Toasted one side of the bread and sprinkled some Nestlé's Toll House mini chocolate chips. Every mother's secret weapon."

Russell smiled from ear to ear. "This is the most fun I've had in a long time!"

But I shudder even today thinking about it.

That night, my bedtime prayer with Scott was more heartfelt than ever. My only boy . . . a special blessing to me.

Scott the Strong-Willed and Kate the Compliant became our professors in raising healthy children. To do so, Barb and I had to learn to balance affirmation with expectation, relationship with rules, love with leadership, cheering with coaching, discipleship with discipline, tenderness with training and teaching, and mercy and grace with justice and consequences.

We learned that good parenting requires immense selflessness marinated in lots of time, effort, patience, and understanding, all undergirded by persistent and never-ending prayer! And we still had the potential perils of adolescence ahead of us!

32

The Gambler

AFTER OUR TRADITIONAL weekly *pain perdu* breakfast, I'd often take the kids on hospital rounds. They loved going, and the nurses and patients enjoyed seeing them. Arriving home one Saturday, I found Barb making up the guest bedroom. "Somebody coming to visit?" I asked.

"I'm not sure," she answered.

"Meaning?"

"I just have a sense that we may have a surprise visitor. But if not, I enjoy having the room looking nice."

At that moment, our doorbell rang.

"I'll get it," Scott yelled as I helped Barb make the bed. We heard Scott talking with someone, and the voices grew closer.

"Well, my room's ready!" boomed Frank Crespo as he entered the bedroom. He was, as usual, in scrubs and unshaven.

We turned to see he was disheveled, and his eyes were bloodshot.

He looked down. "If possible, I need a place to stay for a day or two."

"How about a cup of coffee?" Barb asked. She sent the kids out to play, and the three of us sat out on the back porch.

"She threw me out!" Frank began.

"Who?" Barb asked.

"Nan," he said, referring to his wife. "I was out playing poker most of the night and got home just before dawn. When she got up, I had to share the bad news."

"Bad news?" I asked.

Frank nodded and took a big gulp of the strong, black coffee. "Just like I like it, Barb. Not Cuban, mind you. But not bad. May I smoke?"

Barb did not like tobacco at all but agreed since we were on the back porch. She stood to get a small bowl for him to use as an ashtray.

"Thanks." He took a puff and continued. "When Nan got up, I had to tell her I had lost our house."

"What?" Barb exclaimed.

"Believe it or not, I gambled our home. I had one of the best hands ever—a straight flush—a surefire winner. But I was topped and lost. Only one possible hand could beat me, a royal flush, and the odds against that are half a million to one. If you are dealt twenty hands of poker every night, you'd only have one chance to draw a royal flush in eighty-nine years. But that's what happened."

He took a long draw. "We have to be out by Monday night. Nan went berserk. She started screaming and yelling and demanded I leave. When she grabbed a knife, I left. I was in my car, and she began carrying out my clothes and suits and throwing them in the yard. I loaded as much as I could in my Porsche, but there's not enough room. Anyway, I need two things, if possible."

"We'll help any way we can," I said.

"I'd like to borrow your truck to get the rest of my stuff off the front lawn before it rains, and I could use a place to crash for a couple of days."

I looked at Barb, who smiled and said, "Frank, I sensed someone would need a place. It's ready for you."

She knew. She just knew. Amazing.

"How about y'all take Walt's truck? I'll follow and talk a bit with Nan. Would that be okay?"

Frank nodded and stubbed out his cigarette.

"I know you're not a person of prayer, Frank," I said, "but Barb and I are. Would it be okay if we prayed for you?"

Frank nodded and bowed his head. I don't remember what we prayed, but I remember the sweetness of Barb's prayer for Frank and Nan, for forgiveness and wisdom.

"Frank," Barb said softly, "I know this will work out. I *know* it."

Frank and I picked up his belongings scattered across the front lawn. Barb stayed with Nan for a while. That afternoon, I assisted him in surgery, and when we arrived home, Nan was there. The kids were at the Adamsons', and Barb had prepared a splendid meal so we could talk in private. We suggested that they stay apart that night, Nan in their home, Frank with us, and invited them to attend church with us the next day, which they did—the first time that they had darkened the door of a church for a long time. Afterward, we went to lunch at the Cuban restaurant. They seemed to be warming up to each other.

Just then, another Cuban couple walked up to us. The man was tall and handsome, and the petite woman on his arm a blonde beauty. Frank bristled, but before he could move or say a thing, the man spoke. "Crespo, Gabriella and I were on the other side of the restaurant and saw you. And Gabby said, 'I told you so. Will you listen to me now?'"

Frank and Nan looked confused. No doubt, Barb and I were.

"I told her about my amazing luck Friday night, about how I won your house and how it would be ours on Monday, as soon as you got the title changed."

"I got *so* mad at Jorge, Francisco," Gabby said to Frank. "First, for putting *my* home on the table. I told him if he *ever* did that again, he would be an instant eunuch. Then I told him there was *no* way he was taking the house of my friend Nan and her children. If Nan wants him out, that's fine. But no husband of mine would make a fellow Cubano's wife and children homeless. I also stated in *no* uncertain terms that if he went through with this, even though he says he won it fair and square, he would be, well, how should I say it? Celibate for a long time, or maybe he'd be forced to learn how much attorney he could afford! Anyway, he changed his mind about the house and said we'd go tell you. But I had a feeling. I told him that I thought we'd see you when we were out today—and then you all walked in. I think it's a sign from God, don't you, Francisco?"

Frank could only sit there, stunned. Nan rose and embraced Gabby, kissing her on both cheeks and hugging as they both wept. When Nan stood back, she said, "Thank you, Gabby. For saving my house and maybe my marriage."

Our experience with Frank and Nan, learning about Gabby's intuition, and remembering Barb's premonition about the retirement Ponzi scheme were valuable object lessons for me that taught me to appreciate a woman's subconscious processing power—to take their intuition even more seriously, to value and honor it. As a result, I have had far fewer conversations ending with "I told you so!" Whenever Barb, my daughter, or one of my female colleagues, staff, or patients say, "I just have a feeling" about this or that, I listen very carefully.

33

Patients Know

ONE DAY, A thirty-eight-year-old woman, who had just moved to town, came in complaining of having no periods (called *amenorrhea*) for over a year and having a milky discharge from both breasts (called *galactorrhea*). Her physician was worried about a tumor in her pituitary gland, but a brain MRI and hormonal blood tests were normal. He told her not to worry—that her symptoms would likely go away with time. But she continued to be apprehensive and wanted a second opinion.

"What concerns you the most about this? Any thoughts on what this could be?" I asked.

"You know," she said, "the symptoms began not too long after I started taking a new psychiatric medication called *Navane*. I'm wondering if there might be a connection."

Bingo! I thought. "Absolutely!" I said, explaining that her prescription was in a class of drugs called *neuroleptics* that can cause her exact symptoms. The rather uncommon disorder was called *neuroleptic-induced amenorrhea/galactorrhea*.

We doctors always sense great relief and satisfaction when a patient "gives" us the diagnosis, as they often will, and then offers us the credit for confirming their God-given gift. Women—these sensitive, feeling, intuitive creatures—are crafted this way by their Creator, and part of my job in honoring and cherishing them is to recognize and value their divine design. I learned to appreciate, even seek out, my patients' intuition.

Tamara was a shining example of women's intuition. One morning, she brought in her three-year-old daughter, Addison, who had a high fever that had resolved at home with acetaminophen. The child's exam was normal, so I recommended hydration, fever control, and watchful waiting.

"But I'm concerned, Dr. Walt," Tamara said.

"What bothers you?"

"I think Addie has meningitis."

Meningitis is a life-threatening and highly contagious medical emergency usually caused by a bacteria or virus. A rapid and accurate evaluation by history and exam is critical. I explained to Tamara that Addie didn't have any examination signs of meningitis, her fever was quickly controlled, and she just didn't look sick. She didn't have any of the other common symptoms of meningitis, such as vomiting, headache, sensitivity to light, or a rash.

"Well," Tamara huffed, "she looks sick to me, and I think her neck *is* a bit stiff."

"We have two options. One is for you to watch her at home and call me if she gets any worse. The other is to take her to the hospital ER, where I can do a spinal tap and test her spinal fluid for infection. That's not a risk-free procedure, but it's the gold standard for ruling the diagnosis in or out."

Tamara chose, somewhat reluctantly, to take Addie home to watch and wait.

While making rounds on my patients at the hospital late that afternoon, I heard Dolly's voice over the intercom. "Dr. Larimore, please pick up line two." It was Barb.

"Tamara just called me at home. She says Addie is sicker, and her neck is getting stiffer. I told her to take her to the ER to see you. She's on her way in."

After reexamining Addie and finding everything the same, I could not dissuade Tamara that her daughter had meningitis. She was getting more upset.

Hysterical, my shady side advised.

Be careful, warned my good side. *Intuition. Don't forget it!*

I explained to Tamara the potential risks of infection or bleeding with a spinal tap and how we would work to prevent them. She was visibly relieved and said, "Let's do it." After signing the consent form, she put her hand on my arm. "Dr. Larimore, I'll be praying for you and Addie."

The spinal tap involved having one nurse, Sandi, hold Addie on her side, in a tuck position, which would help open the spaces between the spines of the lumbar vertebrae. I washed her lower back with Betadine and numbed the skin. Then I painlessly inserted a long spinal needle between the spines of the fourth and fifth lumbar vertebrae and into the subarachnoid space, and the fluid flowed freely.

To my relief, the spinal pressure was normal (infection usually increases it), and the spinal fluid looked benign, just like fresh water (whereas with infection, it will be milky or creamy). After the procedure, I carried Addie back to her mother and reassured her that the fluid looked normal, but I would need to wait thirty to sixty minutes for the preliminary results of testing on the spinal fluid, urine, and blood. I finished making rounds and returned to the ER. Ken Byerly was at the doctors' station.

"Just called Sandi down on the pediatric wing for your admission."

"What admission?" I asked, assuming he had admitted another of our patients.

"The little girl with meningitis," he said, pointing to the lab results. "Her urine is clear, and the chest X-ray is normal. But she has an elevated white blood cell count, and her spinal fluid has white blood cells and bacteria." Ken was right, and the spinal fluid culture grew *Streptococcus pneumoniae*, a bacterium we called *pneumococcus*. Doctors these days seldom see this infection as routine immunization has reduced the risk in young children by over 90 percent.

Tamara graciously did not say, "I told you so," despite her what-I-now-call *mama's intuition*. Although we diagnosed the infection very early and could treat it, the disease still caused deafness in one of Addie's ears. In those days, 30 percent of kids with bacterial meningitis developed mild to profound hearing loss.

For a while, I beat myself up. *Why didn't I listen to the mom? What if I had made the diagnosis earlier? Could I have prevented the hearing loss?*

John and I talked about it, and he reassured me I had taken the right path. "With even earlier treatment, the hearing loss can still occur," he reminded me. "And catching it as early as you did likely prevented not only total deafness but other serious complications such as epilepsy, vision loss, mental defects, maybe even a premature death. I'm happy for you, Tamara, and Addie, that things turned out as well as they did, Walt."

Another example of women's intuition was Suzanne. She was a twenty-year-old who just knew "for a fact" that the tender lump she found in her breast was cancer. The actual odds of it being cancer were less than one in a thousand. For almost all women her age, breast lumps, especially painful ones, are benign—either cysts or solid lumps called *adenomas*. In fact, less than seven percent of breast cancer occurs in women under forty years of age. Other than taking hormonal birth control, she had no risk factor for breast cancer. The lump was small, but size doesn't affect the odds something is cancer. Her exam findings didn't make me worry about cancer, but her intuition and insistence bothered me.

By now, I was in tune with intuition, and I did an immediate ultrasound in the office. It confirmed a solid lump. The mammogram showed very dense breasts, which is common in younger women, but no signs of cancer. I knew the only way to convince us both that there was nothing to worry about was to do a biopsy. We used what was then a newer technique called *stereotactic biopsy*. Hamp Sessions, MD, the radiologist, used a mammography machine to create images of the breast tissue from various angles to direct a needle into the lump and retrieve samples.

Only a few days later, we had the diagnosis. To my surprise but not shock, Suzanne had early breast cancer. Dr. Gonzales assisted me with the lumpectomy. There was no evidence of metastasis, so we banished the potentially fatal cancer. She was delighted. I too was more than relieved.

Chalk up another lesson learned for old hardhead. As a result, I would sit down with, question, and then listen, *really* listen, to my patients. In doing so, I have found that most patients will suspect and have read up on their diagnosis. This is even easier now with Google and the internet. But it's been the case for decades. Physician and poet Richard Armour recorded this wisdom in the 1950s:

One thing that is really not difficult, friends,
  Is keeping abreast of new medical trends,
New treatments, new gadgets, new antibiotics,
  New cures for the ailing, including neurotics.
And if you don't learn from attending a meeting,
  Or glancing at journals, though glances be fleeting,
Or talking with colleagues, you'll not be without it,
  For surely your patient has read all about it![1]

In other words, the patient often knows about "it" if the physician will but ask. One of the most important diagnostic questions I have learned to ask is, "So what concerns you the most about this problem?" More times than not, the patient will nail it—especially females.

I now teach the students and residents who study with me that when sailing the choppy waters of difficult symptoms, the storm is calmed when a patient directs us to the port of diagnosis. I was glad to have had multiple "professors" educate me on how to listen to and prioritize their concerns as well as how to explore and understand their perspective. These experiences set the table for my learning to be engaged in joint decision-making with them— patients with whom I'm now able to pray "that you may enjoy good health and that all may go well with you, even as your soul is getting along well."[2]

34

Less Terrible

I WAS FINALLY beginning to both understand and value a woman's intuitive gift as part of her unique design. Even though most women cannot rationally explain their intuition, and even though the gift of intuition is *not* infallible, I've still found it's accurate most of the time not only in my personal life but also in my professional career. In the case of Barb, I realized that her God-given and Spirit-led intuition dovetailed with my blind spots and weaknesses.

As my respect and admiration for Barb's wisdom, intuition, and increasing spiritual maturity continued to grow, I became more alarmed at her discomfort with my long hours and my coming home grumpy. I believed I was doing what I was called to do vocationally as a Christian who just happened to be a family physician. I was receiving deep joy from caring for families physically, emotionally, relationally, and spiritually. It was satisfying to be able to finally support my family after investing twenty-three years in education, paying off school debt, and surviving my horrible investment decision. But was I failing as a husband and father?

I was particularly convicted when Kate told me, "Daddy, we missed you at dinner last night."

"I missed being here."

"I told Mommy I was sad you weren't here. She said that we

couldn't spend our lives waiting for you—that we will include you when you can join us, and we will miss you when you can't."

At that moment, I made a decision. I would make it a priority to be home for dinner as much as possible. Even if it meant going back into the office or hospital after the kids were in bed or waking up earlier the next morning to catch up, I needed to be home more. And not only that, I needed, somehow, to learn how to leave my concerns about my patients and their myriad problems at work—and to quit bringing them home, draped like wet sandbags across my mind and shoulders. However, I had no idea how to do this.

After one particularly long and challenging day, I knew I wasn't in any shape emotionally or spiritually to go home. I called Bill, and he agreed to meet me at a small park at the turnoff to the long driveway to his house. We sat on a bench under a large oak tree where a narrow stream from his farm flowed into Lake Toho.

"You look upset, Walt."

"I am." I confessed to him that Barb and I were having more frequent fights about what our evenings would look like when I arrived home.

"Tell me more."

"Well, as you know, my days in the hospital and the office can be long and stressful. And when I get to the house, I need some space to relax, to veg. No questions or talking—just some processing time by myself."

"So," Bill asked, "what's the problem?"

"When I walk through the door, Barb and the kids instantly want a piece of me. They want to hear about my day. They crave to tell me about theirs. After dinner, they all want to stroll out by the lake. But I desire some *me* space. Without it, I get irritable, and my fuse gets mighty short. Sometimes I just pop off for no clear reason. It worries me that I'm trampling on Kate's and Scott's little spirits and that I risk hardening Barb's heart."

"What do you think the Lord would have you do?" Bill asked.

"I'm not sure. I feel selfish if I take the time I need. But my anger and frustration are not honoring to my kids and my wife and their needs. Barb reminds me again and again that she didn't sign up to be a single parent. She says she needs and expects me to help her out. I think I'm hurting them and myself. I don't know what to do."

Bill reached into his overalls and pulled out his well-worn pocket New Testament. He flipped through the pages until he found what he was looking for. "See if this helps. Paul wrote in 1 Corinthians, chapter thirteen: 'Love is patient, love is kind. . . . It does not dishonor others, it is not self-seeking, it is not easily angered, it keeps no record of wrongs. . . . It always protects, always trusts, always hopes, always perseveres. Love never fails.'"[1]

I shook my head and felt annoyed. "That Scripture is beautiful, but I don't see how it helps!"

"Maybe it would," Bill counseled, "if you could love and honor all four of you—Barb, Kate, Scott, and *yourself.* If you could be kinder and less irritable, then wouldn't that protect their needs and your emotional health?"

"Sounds great, but how do I do that?"

"I may have an idea," he said. "This little park where we're sitting now, you pass it every day when you're going home, correct?"

I nodded.

"Why not stop here for a few minutes? Sit on this bench, and picture yourself dumping all your stress and anxiety, your fears, and your burdens into this stream. Take them off your shoulders, discard them here, and let the current take them away. Think of it as spiritual breathing. Exhale the bad and inhale the positive. Get rid of any negativity. The Bible says that if we confess our sins to him—if we unload them to God—he 'will forgive us our sins and purify us from all unrighteousness.'[2] Think of exhaling as discarding and dumping, and then inhale God's goodness."

I was beginning to see his point.

"Breathe in the good air, the Holy Spirit. Ask him to fill you and renew you. In Ephesians, Paul commands Christians to be filled with the Holy Spirit.[3] The Greek word translated *filled* means "to be controlled and empowered." The Bible also says that when we are filled with the Spirit, instead of being fussy and grumpy, we'll sing and make music from our hearts to the Lord, and we'll be able always to give thanks to God for everything.[4] Walt, you could do this every day on your way home—right here. It wouldn't take five or ten minutes. I bet you'd arrive in a much better mood."

"I'd sure like that!"

"I bet Barb and your kids would also." Bill laughed. "When we're filled with the Spirit, the fruit of the Spirit will pour out of our souls. That fruit is love, joy, peace, patience, kindness, goodness, faithfulness, gentleness, and self-control.[5] If you spiritually breathe out, confess and blow out the bad, and inhale, take in the fullness of his Spirit, then his fruit will fill you and overflow to others—your patients and your family."

"Bill, I like that advice a lot. I do. But I have a question."

"Shoot."

"Why do you say *fruit* and not *fruits*? There are nine of them, right?"

"It's not me. That's what the Bible says. I think the answer is in the punctuation."

"What do you mean?"

"Well, the verse says, 'The fruit of the Spirit is love.' I like to think there's a colon after the word *love*. So the *eight* 'fruits'—joy, peace, patience, kindness, goodness, faithfulness, gentleness, and self-control—are manifestations of the primary fruit of the Spirit, which is love." He opened his Bible and pulled out an old piece of paper. "Found this a long time ago, and I think of it this way." He began to read:

Joy is love singing; it's love's consciousness.
Peace is love resting; it's love's confidence.

Patience is love enduring; it's love's habit.
Kindness is love's true touch; it's love's activity.
Goodness is love's character; it's love's quality.
Faithfulness is love's habit; it's love's quantity.
Gentleness is love's self-forgetfulness; it's love's tone.
Self-control is love holding the reins; it's love's victory.[6]

Bill folded the paper. "Not sure where that came from, but I love it."

"I do too," I said.

"Walt, I've learned that true love, Christian love, agape love, is the queen of all the graces. It is the Son light, S-O-N light, that feeds and reflects off all the other fruit."

"Makes sense. I'm reading Brother Lawrence's book *The Practice of the Presence of God*. He says that the whole substance of religion is faith, hope, and love. In the practice of these we become united to the will of God. All things are possible for the one who believes, less difficult for the one who hopes, easier for the one who loves, and still easier for the one who perseveres in the practice of them.[7]"

"I guess that's why the Bible says that love never fails," Bill commented. He flipped a few pages in his Bible. "Here it is in 1 Corinthians. 'And now these three remain: faith, hope and love. But the greatest of these is love.'"[8] Bill closed his Bible and smiled. "Walt, I've seen you grow a great deal since we first met a few years back. You may not see it, but I do."

"What?" I asked.

"You're getting better—as a spiritual man, a husband, and a father."

I chuckled. "Maybe I'm just getting a little less horrendous."

Bill laughed. "I like that. The many ministeps of becoming a man of God just mean getting a little less terrible each day! But that's positive growth, isn't it?"

That advice changed me forever; it was deep wisdom saturated in rich life experience.

PART SIX

35

The Best Medicine

I REMEMBER A PROFESSOR in medical school always saying, "Laughter is the best medicine." Behind his back, we students would snicker, "Unless you're having angina, then nitroglycerine is the best medicine!" or "Unless you have type 1 diabetes, then insulin is the best medicine!" or "Unless you go to Tulane, then transferring to LSU is the best medicine!"

The professor taught us that laughter produced biochemicals in our bodies that help relieve stress and enhance physical and mental health. It made sense to me that it could also improve emotional and relational health—even spiritual health.

The Bible teaches this in Proverbs 17:22, where the wise King Solomon recorded, "A cheerful heart is good medicine, but a crushed spirit dries up the bones." But in Ecclesiastes 7:3, he also said, "Sorrow is better than laughter, for by a sad countenance the heart is made better."[1] *Hmm,* I thought. *Is an occasional good cry better than a hearty laugh?*

In practice, I came to appreciate the healing value of both laughter and tears. But truth be told, a great laugh *could* calm anxiety, reduce pain, and bring sunshine to a soul. Someone once said,

"Laugh when you can. It's cheap medicine."[2] And, I would add, effective.

Some of my fondest memories are sharing gut-busting laughs with my partner, John. We loved telling jokes and puns with each other. It wasn't unusual for hilarity to enter the exam room. I found that people who could chuckle and stay lighthearted seemed to do better with life's everyday challenges.

One day, a young mother related an anecdote about her four-year-old son. The child had been eager to hold his new one-month-old sister, but she had to tell him repeatedly, "You cannot pick up your sister because you are too little."

"Then just yesterday," she said, "during my daughter's nap time, I was shocked to see him walk into the room where I was folding clothes, proudly carrying his sister. All I could think to say was, 'How'd you get her?' He told me he had climbed over the side of her crib and managed to lift her out and carry her to me. And all this with not a cry from the baby. I was still in shock and said, 'Why did you disobey me?' He said, 'Mom, I didn't disobey. You said I couldn't pick up my sister because I'm too little. I wanted to show you I could.' He held her up. 'See, I can.'" She laughed and added, "I guess I've learned there are times to say 'cannot' and times to say 'may not.'"

"Or 'will not'!" I added. We had a great laugh.

On occasion, a patient would provide me a giggle and not know about it. A fourteen-year-old female track athlete came for a preparticipation sports physical. She threw the discus, javelin, and shot put. She was a short, yet very muscular young woman. During the neurologic examination, while seated on a rolling stool in front of her, I asked her to stand on one foot.

Looking bewildered, she asked, "Which one?"

I answered, "Either, it doesn't matter." She stepped on top of my left foot with both of hers and balanced with no difficulty.

Trying not to cry out, I said, "That's great! Please be seated," as I struggled to keep the tears from forming in my eyes.

The student responded, grinning from ear to ear, "Do you want me to stand on the other one, Doc?"

John and I had a great laugh when he told me the story of a forty-year-old man who suffered chronic, severe joint pain from rheumatoid arthritis he'd had since childhood. This day, one of his knees had flared up, and he came in for an injection of steroid and anesthetic—a procedure that would usually give him several months of reprieve. Afterward, the concerned patient asked John if he could tap dance after this treatment.

"I don't see why not," John replied.

The patient let out a hearty laugh and said, "That's wonderful because I never could before!"

John said he had a somewhat embarrassed smile as he realized that there is much good medicine in a joke.

Another day, I watched John and Judy exit an exam room, laughing about something his patient Joan had said. The patient, still in the room, although ill, was also laughing. In response to my inquiring expression, John explained.

"Joan has a mild case of food poisoning. I asked her where she had eaten."

From inside the room, Joan chimed in, "I told him in no uncertain terms that it was *not* my husband's cooking!"

"Being ever the objective scientist," Judy added, "Dr. John said, 'Well, it could be his cooking.'"

Joan was laughing as she added, "So I told the good doctor there was no way *at all* because he's never cooked a meal in his entire life!"

One day, a young mother and her infant presented as an unscheduled appointment, what we called a *walk-in*, with a complaint of diaper rash. I had attended the youngster's birth only a few weeks earlier. On examination, I discovered the infant not only had a diaper rash from a fungus but also had oral thrush. After explaining to the mom that the same yeast caused both, she laughed and said, "So I guess he has butt-and-mouth disease." The staff all had a laugh about this over coffee together. Judy said, "Maybe we could call it the *start-to-finish fungus*." I picked up the ball, saying, "No, let's call it the *buccal-and-bottom condition*." John, not to be outdone, quipped, "Why not the *dentate-to-derrière disorder?*"

We also learned that smiles could be created with more than jokes. Often, after administering an injection to a young patient, I would suggest that the parent treat the child to a milkshake. Sometimes, I'd even write it as a prescription, to the delight of most of the children.

One grandmother told me that after taking her four-year-old grandson to Joanie's for the chocolate milkshake I had prescribed, the child refused to drink it.

"Why?" she had asked.

"Because I don't like chocolate milkshakes!" the child replied.

"Then why did you let me buy it?" she asked.

The sincere and tearful answer was, "Because Dr. Walt said you should buy it."

Another sure smile inducer was Pixie Dust. Small clear-glass flasks of the glitter-like sparkling particles sold at the Disney Parks represented the magical sprinkles used by Tinker Bell to help kids fly if they thought happy thoughts. I used it to help children heal with happy thoughts and always had a vial available. One day, a seventeen-year-old girl presented with a severely painful heel injury she suffered while cheerleading. When I entered the room, she was crying with her mother's arm around her.

"Is it your foot?" I asked.

"It's her heart," her mother answered.

The girl sniffled and looked up at me with tear-filled eyes. "I've broken my foot before *the* most important social event in the universe."

Her mom smiled. "It's *the* big high school dance. It would be her first."

The good news was that X-rays showed no fracture or dislocation, and I diagnosed a simple bone bruise.

"Give me a moment," I said. "I have some treatments guaranteed to get you on your feet and dancing."

The girl's eyes widened. I left the room to allow her tears to be treated with her mother's hug. I returned with a well-padded heel cushion and lace-up ankle brace that both fit comfortably into her shoe. "I'm not done yet," I told her. "You probably know that Dr. John and I care for several characters at Disney."

She smiled.

"Yep. Mickey, Minnie, Goofy. They've all been here. But my favorite patient is Tinker Bell. I think she's one of my smallest, along with Jiminy Cricket."

The young lady and her mother laughed.

"In fact, the last time she was here, she left me some of her magic Pixie Dust for situations just like this one." I reached into a pocket of my white coat and pulled out the enchanted flask. I pulled off the cork and shook a bit of the glitter into my palm.

Her eyes widened like saucers.

"Here are the magic words Tinker Bell said I must always use along with her dust." As my hand circled over her foot and then released a small shower of the legendary remedy, I exclaimed, "Abracadabra, Rumpelstiltskin, Cinderella, get well!" She laughed, and I then helped her onto her feet. Her smile spread from ear to ear as she gingerly began to walk.

"It's better!" she blurted, obviously delighted. "Oh, thank you, Dr. Walt. You're a miracle worker!"

My declaration to this patient that Dr. John and I cared for Disney characters was accurate. Many Disney cast members lived in the western areas of Kissimmee that were close to the theme parks. The most common problems we treated were skin diseases such as folliculitis, impetigo, or cellulitis—all infections related to wearing their hot costumes in the stifling heat and humidity.

A surprise to me, however, was how many suffered traumas because of aggressive parents who demanded pictures taken specific ways or who were not willing to wait in line and would grab, push, or even punch the characters. Bruises and contusions were common, and there was the occasional fracture. I saw the most injuries among the Mickeys and Minnies, followed by Goofy, and a smattering of others. Fortunately, during the late '80s and early '90s, the costumes were redesigned to be lighter and cooler, the time the characters spent in the heat was reduced, and they designated cast members to escort each character and protect them.

Through the years, the magical powers of the Pixie Dust almost always resulted in laughter or, at the very least, in big smiles that contributed to healing. I thought it a delight to practice in a specialty where caring for an aching heart, soul, or spirit is at least as important as treating a bruised body.

36

A Rich Man

AFTER SPENDING HIS LIFE in the jungles of South America, teaching, preaching, and ministering, William returned to Kissimmee to medically retire and teach at Florida Christian College at age seventy-two.[1] What he called *a considerable thorn in the flesh*[2] had precipitated his return. Several of his ancestors had suffered and died from congestive heart failure. In his case, chronic Chagas cardiomyopathy—damage to his heart muscle by the parasite *Trypanosoma cruzi*, which also damaged his kidneys—compounded his condition.

Because of William's frequent need for medical care, I saw him often, and we became good friends. He was a man of unpompous faith and unadorned words. He had few worldly goods and no earthly estate of any consequence. Many would consider his career unpretentious, even unsuccessful. I found him, however, overflowing with practical life experience and real-world wisdom; he was a veritable treasure trove of intelligent insights and sagacious stories. He credited his acumen to his personal relationship with the Lord, combined with rich spiritual growth experiences, and decades of studying and memorizing the Scriptures, which he cherished.

The moments I spent with him were always rewarding and too short. His timing was invariably impeccable. He seemed to arrive at the office whenever John and I felt discouraged or down—whenever we needed encouragement, blessing, or teaching. John would observe, "It seems when the students are ready, the professor will come." And we fretted more about his physical health than he did.

William always told us he thought we lived in a society with too many luxuries and that most modern folks had forgotten the purity of the basics and simplicity. He loved to say that America had too much fast food, too many fast lanes, too many shortcuts, and too much instant gratification. He was fond of relating that he thought it appropriate the United States had a mountain called *Rushmore*. He encouraged us to differentiate between what most people consider to be wealth—money, securities, houses, possessions, positions, and power—and what he felt made up true riches—relationships and service; wisdom and worship; love, joy, and peace; a lifetime of meaningful memories; and an abiding faith through it all.

I cared for him for three years until, at age seventy-five, he found himself in the hospital with complications stemming from an enlarged prostate that had obstructed his bladder. I drained his bloated bladder and brought his heart and kidney failure into equilibrium, but his prostate needed attention beyond my skill level. I asked Frank to drop by and provide a consultation. Frank would tell me, "People who can't pee always want to see me!" He'd laugh and add, "I'm a poet and don't even know it."

Sandi, who was caring for William that day, told me what happened during their morning visit. Dr. Crespo pompously entered the room while William and his wife, Beth, were praying over their breakfast. Rather than interrupting—as would be his usual approach—Frank stood quietly by. When William looked up, he apologized for making Frank wait.

"Humph," scoffed Frank, regarding William's full liquid diet. "If that was all I had to eat, I don't think I'd feel very thankful."

William smiled and replied, "Well, it is enough." His wife, Beth, nodded in agreement. Then he said, "I'm pleased to meet you, Dr. Crespo. Dr. Walt has told me so much about you. I'm glad you came by this morning because I want to tell you about a dream I had last night."

Sandi said Frank looked amused.

William gazed out the window across the neighboring field as he related his dream: "It began with light and beauty all around me, and I felt so peaceful. Then I heard a soft, warm voice declare to me, 'The richest man in Kissimmee will die tonight.'" He turned his brown eyes to look at Frank. "I rarely remember dreams. But this one was so vivid. Could it be a side effect of one of the medications you or Dr. Walt are giving to me? If so, fine. But if not, I need to figure out what the Lord's trying to say to me."

Sandi told me later that Frank appeared to be disconcerted, and for a moment, he was speechless. Then he answered softly, "No, sir. It's *not* the medicines, of that I'm sure. But let's take a look at what we can do something about—your prostate problem."

Frank performed a thorough history and exam. He explained to William and Beth that he recommended discharge from the hospital with an indwelling catheter from his bladder connected to an external bag attached to his upper leg. This would allow his prostate to rest, and at a follow-up visit, they could discuss operative options.

When he left, William turned to Sandi and said, "I've heard Dr. Crespo is one of the better-off physicians in town."

Sandi nodded her head, smiling, and said, "You could certainly say that!"

"I'm still hoping it's a medication and not a prophecy," he added.

As I found out later, William's dream reverberated in Frank's mind all morning. *Die tonight?* he thought. *Rubbish! Absolute rubbish!* He felt the best thing to do was forget about it—but he couldn't. It plagued him the entire day. He wondered about the substernal chest pain he'd had the week before during another distressing fight with Nan and the recurrent heartburn he had experienced during his most recent malpractice trial. Could these signs be a warning of something more serious? His thoughts tormented him throughout the day. After his last patient, he jumped in his Porsche and raced to my office.

Jean Parten, our receptionist, came back to tell me Dr. Crespo had entered the office unannounced, demanding and expecting us—as he usually did—to drop everything to examine his malady of the day. He was waiting in an exam room, obviously distressed. Before I examined him, he told me the whole story.

It was unusual for Frank ever to exhibit fear or uncertainty. I did a complete checkup. Apart from the smoker's rhonchi, which cleared with a cough, and his being overweight, the results were normal. With that reassurance sloughed aside, he demanded a chest X-ray, blood count, and an electrocardiogram. I quickly performed them all, and they were all within normal limits.

I thought to myself, *Other than your tobacco, alcohol and drug abuse, chronic stress, persistent anxiety, recurrent dyspepsia, dysfunctional family relationships, misplaced priorities, distinct spiritual needs, and possible masked depression, you're fine.* But I only dared to say, "I don't see any acute dangers, Frank; however, it wouldn't hurt to take care of yourself physically *and* spiritually."

He seemed reassured but wanted to be certain. "Cut to the chase," he said sharply. "What's the bottom line?"

I sensed his apprehension and tried to calm him: "Frank, there is no way you will die tonight. However, if you don't stop smoking and drinking and begin to take care of yourself—" I began the admonishment, but he didn't allow me to finish.

Having received the reassurance he had come for, and after having snippily silenced the sermon, he muttered, "Thanks, Walt. I appreciate the help." Then he left, confident that his health was as permanent as his considerable skills and wealth. But to me, it embarrassed him to have been, as he later told me, "so foolishly upset by a decrepit and debilitated man's delusional dream."

The phone call came late that night. It took a moment for me to wake up as I heard the distress in the voice on the other end of the line. "Dr. Larimore, I can't believe it. I woke up and found him dead. He wasn't breathing. He didn't make any noise. He didn't even wake me. He died in his sleep. When I dozed off, he seemed to be sleeping so peacefully. Now, he's gone."

"Nan? Is this you?"

"No, Dr. Walt. This is Beth. William has gone to the Lord."

I was astonished. At first, I couldn't believe it. William had seemed stable when I discharged him from the hospital that afternoon. Then I remembered his dream and his vivid prediction. Indeed, the richest man in Kissimmee had graduated to glory that night.

37

A New Man

ABOUT SIX MONTHS after William passed away, Frank and I shared a meal at the Cuban café. He confessed how he had been searching for significance in many ways—surgery, drugs, lavish homes and cars, alcohol, and partying—always, as he said, "Looking for love in all the wrong places. Everything in which I've tried to find meaning or worth or gratification has left me empty. If it wasn't for surgery, I'm not sure I'd have a reason to live." He took a sip of coffee. "There was a rock song about a guy who couldn't get any satisfaction. That's me, though I've tried, and I've tried, and I've tried, and I've tried." He sighed. "But it's nothing but disappointment—unending unhappiness and emptiness. I feel like part of me is dying. I pray that God will either take me or fix me."

His eyes misted—an astonishing occurrence in and of itself for such a macho Cuban man. It was a sweet, precious moment. I said a quick prayer, asking for wisdom and guidance. A Bible verse sprang up in my mind. "Frank, if I could tell you everything that I think God would want to say to you in one sentence, would you be interested?"

"Yes!"

I pulled out a pen, scribbled a verse on a napkin, and said, "'For the wages of sin is death, but the gift of God is eternal life in Christ Jesus our Lord,'[1]" and handed Frank the napkin. "Let me explain. Wages are what we get paid, what we deserve for what we do. If you were not paid for an operation or procedure, that would not be fair or right, would it?"

He shook his head.

"The Bible says that when we do wrong, when we stray away from God's best for us, that we are due a payment, a compensation, and that wage is the death of any relationship with him."

Frank wryly smiled. "Well, I've sure done a lot of wrong things!"

"Everyone has, Frank. In fact, the Bible says, 'All have sinned and fall short of the glory of God.'[2] You're not alone. Because of our mistakes and our sinful nature, every single one of us has separated ourselves from God and his plan for us."

"Which is what?" Frank asked.

"Jesus told us, Frank. He was comparing himself and his plan for us to Satan's plan for his people. He called Satan a thief, and in one of my favorite quotes of Jesus, he said, 'The thief comes only to steal and kill and destroy; I have come that they may have life, and have it to the full.'[3] Frank, he wants you to have a life to the full—to find true meaning and abundance. He's the source of the satisfaction you've been seeking."

Tears began to form in his eyes. "I don't even know what happiness would look like."

"That's exactly what the Bible means when it says, 'the wages of sin is death.' That's the bad news. But there's good news. It also says that 'the free gift of God is eternal life.'[4]"

"But isn't eternal life just pie in the sky by and by?" Frank asked. I could see he was dead serious.

"That's a great question, Frank. When Jesus was praying, he said, 'Now this is eternal life: that they know you, the only true God, and Jesus Christ, whom you have sent.'[5] So eternal life doesn't begin after we die, but it starts with a personal relationship with God that starts in this life. We can know him. He'll walk with us, teach us, and guide us. We *can* find satisfaction and meaning. I know I have."

He was contemplating what I was saying as he took a sip of his Cuban coffee.

"The good news of the Bible is that although we are each condemned to death, God has a gift for us: eternal life in Christ Jesus the Lord. Does this make sense?"

He nodded.

"Frank, here's the entire message of the Bible in a few words. We have all done wrong and have earned separation from him forever. Jesus is the only solution to our predicament. We begin a personal relationship with him by admitting we have done wrong, receiving his gift of forgiveness and eternal life, and starting a new life that is full and meaningful by trusting in him."

Frank smiled. "It sounds like you're saying, 'God loves us, we broke up with him and left him, then Jesus woos us back.'"

"I couldn't say it better, Frank. Jesus said, 'I am the way and the truth and the life. No one comes to the Father except through me,'[6] but he also said, 'No one can come to me unless the Father who sent me draws them.'[7] You have to decide if he's calling you and then if you'll accept his proposal."

He looked down as tears streaked his cheeks. "I'm ready, Walt," he whispered. He bowed his head and prayed to ask Christ to enter his life. When he said, "Amen," and raised his head, his eyes radiated, and his smile dazzled. He was a new creature—a new man. "I feel fresh," he whispered.

"You are, Frank. The Bible says that when we confess our sins to God—when we admit we are wrong and turn away from wrongdoing—then 'he is faithful and just to forgive us our sins and to cleanse us from all unrighteousness.'[8] At this moment, when God looks at you, Frank, he looks at you just as if you've never sinned—not once. You are forgiven, you are clean, and you are now his child."

His eyes widened a bit. "Really?"

"The apostle John wrote, 'Yet to all who did receive him, to those who believed in his name, he gave the right to become children of God.'⁹ So if we are both children of God, since we now share the same heavenly Father, then we are—"

"Brothers!" he exclaimed. "Wow!" His ear-to-ear smile radiated. "How do you like having a Cuban brother, Walt?"

The next year had its ups and downs for Frank. The old Frank still haunted him, but over time, the new Frank began to shine. He would come over to the house for Bible study and prayer. He even began praying with some of his patients before surgery. It was a joy to see his spiritual life slowly blossom and bear fruit.

About a year later, Frank showed up at our practice unannounced. "Do you have a minute? Can we sit in your office?" He looked worried, and I was concerned as we sat.

He gazed out the window and sighed. "I just received a phone call from a neurosurgeon I've seen in Tampa. I've been having some neurological symptoms. I worried it was from the years of smoking or drinking or partying. You know, Walt, a few too many neurotoxins."

He chuckled, and I smiled.

"He ordered a brain scan. It turns out there's a large tumor in my brain stem. He knows the tumor type without even having to do a biopsy. It's one that won't respond to radiation or chemotherapy. Surgery's my only option, and the possibility of it killing me isn't small."

His eyes filled with tears. "It's either a slow, uncomfortable death or try surgery. It may not work, but it's the only chance I have at a cure and continuing as a surgeon. Walt, you know I'm a great surgeon, and I love surgery—it's both my calling and my gift. I couldn't go on if I couldn't do surgery. Believe it or not, I've been praying about this—talking to Nan and the kids—a lot. Walt, I've put my affairs in order. I will say some goodbyes—a few, not too many. And I'm going forward with the surgery."

"I can't imagine how difficult a decision this must be."

"The hardest thing I've done in my life. But my family and I are at peace with it. Best of all, I sense the Lord agreeing." He pulled out a piece of paper. "The priest gave me this after my last confession."

I unfolded it and read, "Yes, and I shall rejoice. For I know that through your prayers and the help of the Spirit of Jesus Christ this will turn out for my deliverance, as it is my eager expectation and hope that I shall not be at all ashamed, but that with full courage now as always Christ will be honored in my body, whether by life or by death. For to me to live is Christ, and to die is gain."[10] I handed it back, and he replaced it in his scrub shirt pocket.

"Frank, do you believe that?"

He nodded. "With all my heart, Walt." He paused, then asked, "Will you pray for me?"

"Absolutely, Frank. Of course. When's the surgery?"

"Tomorrow morning. I'm heading over to Tampa this evening."

This was classic Frank. Decide and move forward. "How about we pray now?" He nodded, and we held hands and prayed. I asked for guidance for the surgeon and peace for Frank and the family. He thanked the Lord for our friendship and prayed for healing and that he would come home soon. We said, "Amen," and shared tears and a long hug.

"See ya soon," he said as he left.

———

Frank never woke up after surgery—at least not on this side of eternity. He was instantly transported home to a mansion[11] the Lord had prepared for him from before he was formed in the womb or born[12]—a place with ultimate joy and satisfaction, where "he will wipe every tear from their eyes, and there will be

226

no more death or sorrow or crying or pain. All these things are gone forever."[13]

I was grateful the Lord answered Frank's prayer for healing—for he was completely healed the day of his surgery. He left this globe a far richer man than he had ever been on it. I look forward to seeing him again "soon," at least as the Lord counts "soon-ness."[14]

I miss my friend.

38

Extraordinary Birthdays

AT 5:00 A.M., two hours before sunrise, and with the lights of my old truck turned off, Barb and I glided up the driveway of the Hartmans' home. It was August 27, the clear skies blazing with countless twinkling stars. We had awoken to a comfortable 75-degree Wednesday. I had been on call for the night, and since we had no patients in the hospital, which was unusual, I knew that John would sleep in.

"I hope Cleta remembered to leave the back door unlocked," Barb commented as we exited the truck, being careful not to slam the doors and give away our arrival. I reached into the pickup's bed and lifted a covered basket, and we crept around the house. The door creaked as Barb opened it, and we tiptoed into the kitchen. Cleta had left the hood light on over the stove and had set out the utensils we would need. The light provided just enough illumination for us to prepare our surprise—fresh-squeezed Florida orange juice, eggs Benedict with hollandaise sauce (which had become a favorite of ours during medical school in New Orleans), fresh fruit, and piping hot dark-roast Community coffee from our hometown of Baton Rouge.

"Drats!" Barb exclaimed. "I forgot the flowers. You get the cake ready. I think I saw some flowers blooming on Cleta's front porch." She dashed out before I could object, so I placed forty candles on the stir-and-frost cake Barb had baked. The Duncan Hines box read, "The Perfect Size," and it was!

Barb returned, holding a "borrowed" yellow gerbera daisy, which she deposited in a small vase. While lighting the candles, Barb said, "Remember what happened on my birthday?"

"I do," I said, recalling how I had let Scott use a match to light the candles on his mother's cake. Although he was very slow in lighting them all, he determined to do it with one match and with no help. His strong will persisted despite second-degree burns on several fingers. I had to take him to the office to treat him with burn cream.

We each picked up a loaded breakfast tray, Cleta's with the flower and John's with the brightly lit cake, and tiptoed to their bedroom door where Barb whispered, "Ready?"

I nodded, and we began singing, "Happy Birthday."

John was surprised but delighted. Cleta fluffed their pillows as they sat up, and we placed the trays on their laps as we finished, "Happy fortieth birthday, dear John. Happy fortieth birthday to you!"

"Happy birthday, partner!" I announced.

John laughed. "Well, what a nice surprise!"

"Enjoy it, you two," Barb said as we exited.

"See you at the office!" I added over my shoulder.

Parents who spend most of their time at work and have little or no presence with their children rarely understand how harmful this decision can be to the kids. I know; I was one of those parents. Like most hardworking folks, I sincerely believed that the extra money this effort was bringing would be of long-term benefit to Barb, Kate, and Scott. I didn't see how my not being there was hurting them.

Barb would not let my absence impede the family's pressing on. She'd tell the children, "Dad can't be with us, but we're going ahead without him," and she'd do whatever needed to be done. Three convicting experiences took place that changed my course and the health of my marriage, parenting, and family.

John was concerned about how much of life I was spending away from my brood but wasn't sure how to approach me. Then during one of our morning coffee breaks, he said, "Walt, I have a younger brother whom I'm concerned about. May I ask for your thoughts about him?"

"Sure," I said.

"He's a great guy. Loves his job. Loves his family and his church. My concern is that he's spending far, far more time at work than with his family. It's hurting his wife and children, and I don't think he realizes it. I'm not sure what I should say."

I took a sip of coffee, thought a minute, and responded. "John, just tell him you love him, and tell him your concern. Maybe recommend a resource that would encourage him. But I didn't remember you having a younger brother. What's his name?"

John looked away and whispered, "Walt, I love you. And I'm concerned. My younger brother is you."

I was instantly convicted. I hung my head as he hugged me. "Here's a cassette tape of a presentation by family physician Richard Swenson, MD, titled 'Margin: Restoring Emotional, Physical, Financial, and Time Reserves to Overloaded Lives.' He explains how families are being destroyed by parents—dads in particular— who leave no surplus in their schedule for their kids, and how the terrible effects negatively impact not only the marriage but also the parents' relationship with and the health of the children. It was an encouragement for me. Cleta and I are discussing some changes we need to make. I hope it will be a blessing to you."

The next Tuesday morning, when I pushed the door open at Joanie's Diner for my meeting with Bill, the warmth, smells of breakfast, and heartfelt greeting from Joanie—who, to my considerable pleasure, now considered me a regular—were all pleasing and comforting.

I found my way over to our usual table and began sipping a cup of fresh, steaming-hot coffee while I awaited my mentor. As Bill settled into the booth, we shared pleasantries. Then he asked, as always, "What is the Lord teaching you this week?"

"Well, he convicted me, once again, with my daughter's example and my partner's encouragement."

"How so?"

"When I get up in the morning and prepare coffee for Barb, Kate comes out to the kitchen table and reads her Bible and writes in her journal. One morning she asked me, 'Daddy, do you have your quiet time before I get up?'"

"How did you respond?" Bill asked.

"I thought, *Busted.* I poured another cup of coffee and sat beside her and told her, 'I guess I've just gotten so busy that I don't anymore.'"

"What did she say?"

"She continued to write in her journal and sweetly told me it wasn't a problem and that Jesus still loved me anyway. Then, Bill, she told me that Jesus would wait for me each day to sit with him and have a chat. She added that every morning he had much he wanted to teach her, and she was sure he'd do the same with me. Bill, the Lord used my little girl to correct me."

"What did you do?"

"I joined her. Now, most mornings, we sit and have our quiet times together. It turns out that she was 100 percent correct. Jesus did have much that he needed to say to me and teach me. When I returned to him and his Word, sure enough, he was there."

Bill smiled. "Sounds like your daughter, who, I might add, is also your sister in Christ, has become your accountability partner. What did John do?"

I told him the story, and he said, "John used the same approach with you that the prophet Nathan used with King David. Do you know that story?"

I shook my head no.

He immediately opened his Bible and read me the story. The prophet Nathan presented a case of a man doing wrong, and King David became very angry. Then Nathan said to him, "You are the man!"[1] David was immediately convicted and lamented to Nathan, "I have sinned against the LORD." Nathan replied, "The LORD has taken away your sin."[2]

"Is John your Nathan?" he asked.

I could only nod.

"Look here," he said. "This is how that story starts. Read this."

I read, "The LORD sent Nathan to David."[3]

"I think the Lord sent John to you." He flipped toward the back of his Bible and read, "Do not love the world or anything in the world. If anyone loves the world, love for the Father is not in them. For everything in the world—the lust of the flesh, the lust of the eyes, and the pride of life—comes not from the Father but from the world. The world and its desires pass away, but whoever does the will of God lives forever."[4]

I took a deep breath and let it out. "I'm guessing that spending too much time making money, under the guise of providing for my family, puts me at risk for loving the world or the things of the world more than them?"

Bill answered, "That's a good question to ask of the Holy Spirit. He and his Word are more than capable of guiding you. Like the Bible says, 'Trust in the LORD with all your heart; do not depend on your own understanding. Seek his will in all you do, and he will show you which path to take.'"[5]

The final event that sealed my conviction that I needed to

make some changes occurred on Kate's ninth birthday. We had a simple birthday party with just Barb, Scott, and Kate's best friend, Tina, there to watch her blow out the candles on her cake. We all cheered with each brave attempt, and after several tries, she blew out the last candle.

I was reveling in the evening, totally enjoying the party. I realized that nights like this were few and far between, as I was still allowing the medical practice to take way too much of my time. Although my income was meeting legitimate needs, especially paying off our significant debt, I was living with the delusion that my family needed the money I brought in more than they needed me. I was also beginning to understand that I loved practicing medicine, and it fed some of my ego desires. Fortunately for my family and me, my dad provided a wake-up call par excellence that evening.

My parents called from Baton Rouge to wish Kate a happy birthday. She was the first grandchild for both sides of the family and was the first female born into the Larimore family tree in eighty years. These facts, combined with her cerebral palsy, contributed to the reality that they doted on her more than most grandchildren. Nevertheless, what my father told me that night shook me to my core. After trading some small talk, my dad surprised me by saying, "Well, congratulations!"

I remember furrowing my brow, not having any idea about what he was saying. "For what?" I asked, thinking he must be referring to one of my awards or accomplishments or publications.

"One-half of her life with you is over."

It struck me like lightning. I knew immediately what he was pointing out. One day, Kate would leave home for college. It felt like she had been born just the day before. The first years of her life had flown by.

As the shock began to diminish, a wave of reproof penetrated my spirit. I knew I had not been at home as much as I should. I grasped that the days that had passed would never be recovered. I recognized that nothing I could buy my wife and children could replace me as Barb's husband and my kids' father. I more fully understood what Kate, John, Bill, and my dad were trying to teach me—laboring to gather the unnecessary things of the world was a price not worth it and could break me, my marriage, and my family. I needed to let some good things go, so I might hold on to the best things.

39

Eternal Significance

AT MY NEXT breakfast meeting with Bill, I shared what my father had told me and how his message was impacting me personally and professionally.

"It's a remarkable lesson to learn, especially for men," Bill said. "When I was a young man, I craved significance. Like most guys, I wanted to feel unique, special, and, most of all, successful. Then I came across what I think are two of the most powerful verses in the Bible for men who are pursuing success by investing in worldly ventures—fellows chasing temporal pleasure, possessions, and power. Satan can use these temptations to lure guys away from what's most important—what's eternally significant."

He flipped in his Bible to 1 John 2:16 and said, "The Bible labels the desire for pleasure as the lust of the flesh, the desire for possessions as the lust of the eyes, and the desire for power as the pride of life. It also says these things don't come from the Father but the world. You can see how Satan uses these worldly desires in the way he tempts. He tempted Jesus to turn stones to bread for the pleasure of eating, to worship him to possess all the kingdoms of the world, and to jump from the highest point on the temple in Jerusalem to experience the power of making his Father save him."

"I never thought about it that way," I said.

"Many men covet the applause of the world, of the many, not the approval of the One, the Father. Walt, I think what your daddy was trying to tell you is that he's worried you aren't just striving too much but striving for the wrong things. Things that ultimately won't bring success or satisfaction."

I took a deep breath and slowly released it, realizing Bill was right.

"I have another instruction for you. It came to me when I was a young man. It was a critical moment for me when I realized that the desire for pleasure, possessions, and power is not rooted only in my sinful nature. Think about it. Satan appealed to these exact longings in Adam and Eve *before* they were sinful. Christ had no sin nature, yet Satan tempted him with pleasure, possessions, and power. Some people call those the *pernicious Ps*. I call them the *perfect Ps*. Why? Because God placed these three desires in our hearts, and he wants us to allow him—*not* the world—to fill those desires."

"What? You believe the craving for these things is divinely designed?"

"I do. C. S. Lewis wrote, 'If I desire things that this world can't satisfy, the best explanation is that God made me for another world.'[1] God himself appeals to each of these desires in us! He offers us an eternal kingdom filled with the rewards of pleasure, possessions, and power."

"Where does the Bible say *that*?" I asked.

"One example is in Psalm 16 where it says God will make known to us the path of life and that with him, there is 'fullness of joy' and 'pleasures forevermore.'[2] Jesus taught us to lay up treasures—forever possessions, if you will—in heaven. He also explained about position and authority in heaven. Do you remember the parable of the master who went away? It's such an essential principle that

Matthew, Mark, and Luke all recorded it.[3] A master left his servants with money. When he returned, he called them to learn how they had invested the gifts he'd given to them. To the two servants who multiplied his gifts, he granted power and authority in his kingdom. To them, and only them, he said, 'Well done, good servant! Because you have been faithful in a very little, you shall have authority.'"[4]

Bill looked at his watch. "Gosh, our time is about gone. Can I quickly share an application for you?"

I nodded.

"Satan and the world want to convince us to obtain pleasures, possessions, and power in the present world, but they are like unfillable, cracked flasks that will leak our time, treasure, and talent and leave us empty. God's way is to gain them in the future by letting go of them in the present.

"Think about the disciplines of fasting, giving, and prayer. Fasting is denying the pleasure of eating to gain pleasure in God and getting nutrients from his Word. Giving is denying the possession of money to gain treasure from God. Prayer is setting aside requests for one's own power to receive power from God when the Holy Spirit comes upon you, as the Bible says in Acts 1:8."

He finished his juice and wiped his lips. "I guess if you had to boil down what I'm trying to say, Walt, it's this: God appeals to our human nature, but never to our sinful nature. He places divinely designed desires in each of us. The world and Satan can take these legitimate aspirations that our Creator has implanted in our hearts and tempt us to direct them to unrighteous efforts and goals. Make sense?"

Did it ever! A perfect example of God directing my father, my mentor, his Word, and his Spirit to reprove and correct me. The icing on the cake was a devotional Kate shared with me one morning during our quiet time at the kitchen table.

If we believe in Jesus, it is not what we gain but what He pours through us that really counts. God's purpose is not simply to make us beautiful, plump grapes, but to make us grapes so that He may squeeze the sweetness out of us. Our spiritual life cannot be measured by success as the world measures it, but only by what God pours through us—and we cannot measure that at all.[5]

I knew I needed to spend more time at home and to be a better husband and father—to be tempted less by the allure of the world. I realized that doing so would mean less time in medicine and a significantly reduced income.

After much reflection and prayer, I approached John about the possibility of devoting one afternoon each week for each of my children. My typical schedule included morning rounds at the hospital followed by patient appointments until 5:00 or 6:00 p.m., often followed by dinner at home and then evening rounds or meetings. This schedule left little margin to spend time as a husband to Barb and a dad to Kate and Scott.

John was pleased and supportive. We developed a new arrangement: I would see patients from 9:00 in the morning to 2:00 in the afternoon on Tuesdays and Thursdays. On those days, I'd be able to be home by 3:00. Tuesday afternoons and evenings were for Kate—and her alone; Thursdays were for Scott. With either, I might take them fishing or to get a milkshake, or we might work on a puzzle or play a game or read together. Kate and I would take long walks and have long talks about anything and everything. Scott and I would ride bikes, shoot hoops, or play soccer. Then we would go home and work on their homework together. Barb and I committed to having dates at least a couple of times a month. We had half days at least once every month or two that were just for us, and weekends away two or three times a year.

I had a blast! I got to know and love my wife and children in ways that never could have happened any other way. I learned firsthand that *quality time* occurs only during *quantity time*. By letting go of the unnecessary things of the world I had been working so hard to obtain, I gained some out-of-this-world benefits.

In 1998, Kate, by then twenty years old, and I attended a conference for physicians and their spouses. I had been asked to introduce Dr. Richard Swenson and his wife, Linda, who were teaching a parenting seminar. Just before I was to stand up, Kate asked if she could introduce them instead.

"Why?" I asked.

"Because," she answered, with a twinkle in her eyes, "I want to, and I think I can do a better job!"

I chuckled. Anyway, I'm glad I agreed. She stood and said something like this: "Ladies and gentlemen, throughout my life, I've had many gifts given to me by my parents. Birthday presents, Christmas gifts, Easter favors, graduation mementos, and many more. Although I loved getting them all, I remember very few of them.

"Then my daddy heard a talk Dr. Swenson gave. It's now in a book he's written titled *Margin*. My dad learned that if he wanted me to be as healthy as I could be, he would have to spend time with me—a lot of time. He would need to create margin in his schedule and in his world for me. So he took time away from work and spent every Tuesday afternoon and evening with me as I was growing up."

She looked down at me. "Daddy, you've given me so many gifts, but the most wonderful gift you *ever* gave me was yourself. I'll never forget the memories I have from those days."

She turned to Dr. Swenson and Linda and said, "Dr. and Mrs. Swenson, thank you for teaching my daddy. Because of what you taught *him*, I will never be the same." Facing the audience, she said, "Dr. and Mrs. Swenson are here to teach you today about parenting. I encourage you to listen *very* carefully. And then figure out a way to apply these principles, as my daddy and mama did. You and your kids will never, ever, ever regret it."

Then Kate sat down. I'm not ashamed to tell you that both the Swensons and I had tears rolling down our cheeks. She most definitely "did a better job." And I was so happy I had learned that letting go of worldly expendables to invest in eternal essentials was not only wise but also fruitful—and the dividends are literally out of this world! It was for me a wake-up call—and a new birthday!

40

Graduate with Honors

In March, I celebrated a milestone birthday—my fortieth—and was most mindful of Psalm 90:10: "Our days may come to seventy years, or eighty if our strength endures; yet the best of them are but trouble and sorrow, for they quickly pass, and we fly away." As a result, I prayed as Moses instructed in Psalm 90:12: "Teach us to number our days, that we may gain a heart of wisdom."

I was happy that Jesus balanced this reality with the promise that even amid the endless storms of life, he came that we "may have life, and have it to the full"[1] and that he gives his Holy Spirit to nurture in and through us "love," manifested by "joy, peace, patience, kindness, goodness, faithfulness, gentleness, and self-control."[2]

Bill shared a devotion with me the Tuesday morning of my birthday week. "Today, I want to begin with Isaiah 46:4." He opened his Bible and read, "Even to your old age and gray hairs I am he, I am he who will sustain you. I have made you and I will carry you; I will sustain you and I will rescue you."

He closed his Bible, took a sip of juice, and continued, "Walt, the call to be a follower of Jesus is *not* a one-time event but a life-long transformation involving many mini-steps—hopefully, more forward than backward. It's a journey in which Jesus calls us to let go of our identity based on our gifts, talents, achievements, and social standing. When we do, then we can embrace, hold on to, and bear witness to our new identity in Christ. The uniqueness and distinctiveness of becoming a changed person, a new creature—for our good and his glory. As Jesus told his disciples, 'Anyone who intends to come with me has to let me lead. You're not in the driver's seat—I am. Don't run from suffering; embrace it. Follow me, and I'll show you how.'[3]

"I think this is the bottom line of what I've been trying to teach you: do whatever it takes to do whatever he asks, no matter the cost—then when eternity comes, you will graduate with honors."

I remembered what Clem prayed at every rodeo, that we might "live our lives in such a manner that when we make that last inevitable ride to the country up there, where the grass grows lush, green, and stirrup high, and where the water runs cool, clear, and deep, that . . . our last Judge will tell us that our entry fees are paid."[4]

Thomas Jefferson wrote that all people "are created equal, that they are endowed by their Creator with certain unalienable Rights, that among these are Life, Liberty, and the pursuit of Happiness."[5] I was thinking that the biblical equivalent is that we each have a God-shaped void in our hearts for life, freedom, and the quest for holiness. We aren't divinely designed to be "happy" but are each created to partner with our Creator, who crafted us to love others as he loves us—to serve and be compassionate, honorable, and kind. We are to make a difference living well by discovering both whose we are and who we are—in my case, as a person, a husband, a father, a professional, and a member of my church and community. Only then could I live the life Christ designed for me and designed me for—one that is full and meaningful.

Up to this point, I had been a physician who was a Christian. Now I felt I was becoming at my core a Christian—a follower of Jesus—who just happened to also be called as a physician. I had a long way to go but now felt I was making a good start.

I had arrived at work and was in my private office, enjoying a cup of coffee and meditating on how much I had learned since beginning practice in Kissimmee. I picked up an envelope on my desk marked CONFIDENTIAL. I opened it and read the message from a New York attorney. It seemed too good to be true. He was letting us know that the unscrupulous retirement advisor who had ripped us off in the illegal Ponzi scheme had lost his SEC license and would not be able to cheat others.

Furthermore, the advisor had sat on the board of the bank that lent us the money—which was flagrantly unethical and potentially illegal. As a result, to prevent any possible lawsuits, the bank was willing to cancel our remaining debt in full. Also, we might even receive some funds back. I couldn't wait to call Barb and let her know.

"Hey, Walt!" The greeting interrupted my thoughts. A half-finished cup of coffee sat on my desk as Dan Autrey walked in. "Jean said you were back here. I only have a moment but wanted you to know I'm getting hitched again."

"What! To whom?" I asked. "I wasn't aware you were even dating again!"

"It has all been hush-hush. Turns out my first girlfriend, my high school sweetheart, Glenn Granger, married an Ob-Gyn physician up in North Carolina. He passed a few years back, and we reconnected. Believe it or not, we had been engaged before World War II took us different directions. Anyway, we've been visiting each other here and at her home in Elizabeth City, North Carolina. I've got to get up to the Orlando airport to catch a plane. I want you and Barb to meet her when we come back down here. Gotta go! Keep me in your prayers!" He turned and walked away before I could say a word.

"Quit your daydreaming and finish your coffee!" Judy said as she walked up to my dictation station. "Patients are backing up in the waiting room, which is irritating to Susan *and* Jean. Katie Lockwood's in the treatment room, probably with a broken wrist."

Susan turned the corner and handed me a note. "Clem just called. He's in town for the rodeo and wants to meet for dinner." Handing me a small brown bottle, she added, "This is from Hadlee. It's a juice from Hawaii. She says they make it from, and I quote, 'One of the world's most important healing plants. The healing and cancer-fighting properties have been confirmed by modern scientists.'" Turning the label to better view the small print, she added, "It 'reduces chronic pain, boosts the immune system, prevents colds and the flu, and neutralizes free radicals to ward off other diseases such as arthritis, blood clots, cancer, diabetes, depression, and hypertension.' She says if you sell it here, you'll have fewer patients to see, but you'll make a lot more money and help a lot more people."

We heard a commotion and turned to see what it was. Erin's mother and another nurse, each pulling one of Erin's arms, were dragging her toward Room 6. She resisted every step of the way. "I ain't gonna have no shots! None! This is child abuse!" she screamed. "I'm gonna report you all to the state!"

"God bless us, everyone!" Judy said as we all shared a laugh.

I loved being a generalist and can't imagine not being able to take care of the full spectrum of our patients' and their families' needs for their entire lives. It is a thrill that the limited-care medical specialist misses out on. It reminds me of science-fiction writer Robert Heinlein's character Lazarus Long in the book *Time Enough for Love*:

> A human being should be able to change a diaper, plan an invasion, butcher a hog, conn a ship, design a building, write a sonnet, balance accounts, build a wall, set a bone, comfort the dying, take orders, give orders, cooperate, act alone, solve equations, analyze a new problem, pitch manure, program a computer, cook a tasty meal, fight efficiently, die gallantly. Specialization is for insects. [6]

I can't imagine medicine without prenatal care and geriatric care—without preconception care and end-of-life care—without sports medicine, gynecology, and skin care.

There's just something about being able to care for a child and their entire family, to see them all grow and mature—birth to bereavement, conception to cremation, delivery to departure—from a glorious entry into life to, hopefully, a graduation into glory.

As Kate and I were having our quiet time the next morning, I watched her as she read a few verses in her Bible and thought about them for a moment before furiously scribbling in her journal.

You are *blessed*, I thought. To my surprise, there was no retort. I realized I hadn't heard from my darker side for a while. *No loss there!*

Another thought popped into my mind. For the first time, I began to contemplate the likelihood that my life was at or past the halfway point. How would I take these valuable lessons and apply them for my good and God's glory—to practice, prescribe, and partake in the best medicine the Lord offered? I looked forward to what he would do in and through me, my marriage, my family, and my practice during the next season of my life. I think it was no coincidence that I read these verses that morning:

> The righteous will flourish like a palm tree,
>   they will grow like a cedar of Lebanon;
> planted in the house of the LORD,
>   they will flourish in the courts of our God.
> They will still bear fruit in old age,
>   they will stay fresh and green,
> proclaiming, "The LORD is upright;
>   he is my Rock, and there is no wickedness in him."[7]

I remember wondering why those verses so impressed me on that day. *Flourish like a palm tree?* I thought. *A palm tree Christian? A palm tree physician? Both?* Only time would tell, but it was past time to shake off the past. I expectantly, even eagerly, looked forward to receiving and engaging whatever lay ahead.[8]

Acknowledgments

MANY OF THE CHARACTERS in these tales are still alive and reside in Osceola County, and I'm grateful they consented to have their or their families' stories shared with you. Almost all reviewed their portions of the book for accuracy and completeness. Three with whom I worked during my fifteen years in Kissimmee—Ken Byerly, MD, Sandi Lynch, RN, and Judy Simpson, RN—agreed to represent their respective tribes (our ER physicians, hospital nurses, and office nurses).

I owe an unusually large debt to my family: Barb (my friend for sixty-three years, my best friend for fifty-two years, and my wife-for-life for forty-seven years), son, Scott, and daughter, Kate, for allowing their lives—the trials and thrills, embarrassments and elations, distresses and delights—to be shared with you. As you now know, we are not a perfect family, but we are perfect for each other.

I can't thank John and Cleta Hartman enough for their deep and abiding friendship that has spanned over forty years. The impact they had on me and my family cannot be overstated. I love and admire them more than I can say.

A most special thank you is extended to my dear friend and mentor of over thirty-five years, Bill Judge. One of the editors of this book wrote: "He is a strong presence. I can't decide if he's too saintly. . . . Let me know if it's intentional that his halo is so bright." I responded, "Yes, it's *that* bright!"

Upon reviewing this book, Bill, with his usual humble response, said something like, "I'm not sure I said all those things you say I said." Well, maybe not word for word, but Bill taught me precept on precept, principle after principle, and instruction atop instruction. He was a guide who provided wisdom and conversation always seasoned with salt. His example was a comforting light for my most formative personal, family, and professional years. I love Bill dearly. We continue to visit by phone at least two or three times a month and meet in person every year or two.

Many of the characters described in this work, especially former patients of mine, are composites of one or more real people, and most bear names that are purely fictional—primarily to protect the identity of those on whom the story was based and secondarily to protect those who are either blameless, grumpy, or guilty. Many times, I've changed the name, gender, and age of folks to safeguard their confidentiality and privacy—as they never planned to have their stories divulged in the public square. Therefore, those readers who think they recognize a patient of mine in these pages should consider it a most unlikely happenstance.

Some of the stories in this book are recorded as they happened, or at least how I remember them happening; however, most of the stories did not occur precisely how or when they are written. Artistic license was employed frequently and unapologetically. You see, I'm what is called a *certified storyteller*. Such a designation allows me to use my imagination to rearrange history to improve a story—although every single chronicle is based on a true story. I attempted to write this book in such a way that I might not be disqualified from this self-professed certification. Nevertheless, some readers may question how an extremely busy physician could remember so much detail about so many events from so long ago.

First, many of these stories have been repeated again and again to family and friends as well as at medical lectures and talks literally around the world. They are seared into my and my family's collective memories.

Second, I've also used snippets from a few stories in my bestselling Bryson City series (*Bryson City Tales, Bryson City Seasons*, and *Bryson City Secrets*) and in my health books to catch readers up, where necessary, with past family or professional events.

Third, during a research trip to Kissimmee in the fall of 2019, Jerry and Jennifer Adamson, Allan and Kathy Baker, Bill and Jane Judge, John and Cleta Hartman, Polly Prather, and Edna Thacker spent significant time with Barb and me to refresh our memories, clarify facts, and provide even more stories that will appear in the next book. Since then, Edna has graduated to glory. Oh, how she was looking forward to this book.

As we drove around town and our old neighborhoods, we were warmly greeted by neighbors and friends who still live there. What fun we had speaking with them, walking along the lakeshore, and discovering and visiting the new Brownie Wise park on the shore of Lake Toho.

Finally, and perhaps most significantly, for almost ten of the fifteen years I practiced family medicine in Kissimmee, I wrote more than 160 columns titled *Diary from a Week in Practice* for one of the most widely distributed medical journals in the world, *American Family Physician* (*AFP*). A note from the journal's editor, Jay Siwek, MD, stimulated the idea for these columns. In July 1990, he wrote that he was "seeking contributions that highlight the joys and sorrows, the discoveries and disappointments of day-to-day family practice. We want to capture the intangible heart of family practice—what it means to be someone's family physician and how that special doctor-patient relationship adds to the satisfaction of practicing medicine"[1] and to "highlight the joys and sorrows, the discoveries and disappointments of day-to-day family practice."[2]

I loved Jay's suggestion and submitted sample columns. The next thing I knew, I was a "writer." Well, truth be told, Jay and his amazing editorial staff taught me how to write by their edits, corrections, suggestions, coaching, teaching, and expert guidance. Those columns ran from January 1992 until August 2001. The *AFP* managing editor later wrote, "Walt and his partner, John R. Hartman, MD, rose to the challenge, filling entry after entry with stories of successes, anecdotal remedies and observations, memories of special patients, and moments of crisis and quiet reflection."[3] We were told reader surveys indicated the column was the most read and beloved item in the journal. Many of those old diary entries became important sources of recollection for this book.

I'm grateful to Barb Larimore, Sherry Compton (former rodeo barrel rider and media manager for the ProRodeo Cowboys Association), Lois Johnson Rew (author of *Editing for Writers*[4]), and Katherine Ritz for reading a draft of the manuscript and providing excellent suggestions and edits. I appreciate Anza Bast, archives assistant, Osceola County Historical Society, for providing a fact check of the historical portions of the book, and the *Orlando Sentinel* for providing its archive for my review.

Almost all my books are reviewed for biblical soundness by the elders at the church we are attending at the time the book is written. In that regard, I owe a debt of gratitude to my elder board and pastors at Academy Christian Church in Colorado Springs, Colorado. Thanks especially to Jim Collier, Pastor Richard Crabtree, Al Fritts, Steve McFarland, and David F. Smith for their review and insightful comments.

I'm grateful to my author group—we call ourselves The Stinklings or, in our better moments, The St. Inklings—for encouragement and fellowship during my writing. Thanks, Al, Clarence, Jerry, Larry, and Paul. Thanks also to Don Jones of Studio 9 Commercial Photography for allowing me to use a portrait he took of me. You can see his fantastic photography at tinyurl.com/y3nkdkku.

I'm so grateful to one of the best editors I've ever worked with (who is also a dear friend), Cindy Lambert, who once again depleted a case of red ink pens and incredibly valuable time while making many suggestions that have improved this book dramatically. Then, when I had rewritten the book for the umpteenth time and thought everything was correct and in order, Vicki Crumpton, the executive editor at Revell, read it and made many additional suggestions. Gisèle Mix then provided further edits and proofreading that made the book noticeably easier to read. Thanks, Cindy, Vicki, and Gisèle!

I'm also appreciative of the professional team at Baker/Revell, including but not limited to Erin Bartels, Scott Bolinder, Eileen Hanson, Rod Jantzen, Harrison Meyer, William Overbeeke, Gayle Raymer, Mark Rice, Kelli Smith, Wendy Wetzel, and Janelle Wiesen, who labored to bring *Best Medicine* to fruition.

I appreciate Greg Johnson, the founder and president of WordServe Literary Agency, who not only represents me but has become a friend.

I also owe a debt to Kissimmee and Osceola County and their people. These selected stories represent only a small portion of all that could be told about these special folks—many of whom are descendants of the original Florida settlers—who are a warm, kindhearted, and gentle people. They slowly took me in and welcomed me into *their* community. This book represents a special thank you from me to them—for who they are to me, what they mean to me, and what they've taught me.

As you read about the events that occurred in my medical career, I want you to know that similar books could have been written by most family physicians across America—with, of course, personal and geographic variations. This composition is intended to be more a record of this type of practice (vanishing as it is)—and the personal and professional growth it produced in almost any young physician of that era—than the partial memoir of any single one.

Walt Larimore, MD
Colorado Springs
June 2020

Notes

All URLs were last accessed on April 18, 2020.

Chapter 1 Near Death

1. Romans 7:17–20 MSG.
2. Philippians 4:13 NKJV.
3. Proverbs 16:24 NLT.

Chapter 2 First Day

1. For this chapter, I refreshed my memory with the following: (1) "About Us," Osceola Regional Medical Center, tinyurl.com/qrtz8ph; and (2) Walt Larimore, MD, *Bryson City Secrets: Even More Tales of a Small-Town Doctor in the Smoky Mountains* (Grand Rapids: Zondervan, 2006).

Chapter 3 Gonna Like Him

1. Walt Larimore, *Bryson City Tales: Stories of a Doctor's First Year of Practice in the Smoky Mountains* (Grand Rapids: Zondervan, 2002), 140.
2. For this chapter, I refreshed my memory with the following: John R. Stannard, "A Spiritual Approach to Patients: John R. Hartman, MD, Kissimmee, Florida," *Caring for America: The Story of Family Practice* (Virginia Beach: Donning Company, 1997), 58–59.

Chapter 4 Different Drummers

1. Henry David Thoreau, *Walden* (New York: Thomas Y. Crowell & Company, 1910), 430.

Chapter 5 Back to Nature

1. "About Lake Tohopekaliga," Orlando Bass Guide, tinyurl.com/y5okpv35.
2. Psalm 19:1.
3. Maltbie D. Babcock, "This Is My Father's World," 1901, public domain, Wikipedia, tinyurl.com/y5g4wbhg.
4. For this chapter, I refreshed my memory with the following: (1) "Lake Tohopekaliga," Wikipedia, tinyurl.com/y34fgtv3; and (2) Katherine Long, "Historians Try to Trace Origins of Indian-Named Places," *Orlando Sentinel*, November 16, 1986, tinyurl.com/yxf4qywn (subscription required).

Chapter 6 Cowboy Country

1. For this chapter, I refreshed my memory with the following: (1) an interview with Geech and Connie's daughter, Kathy Baker; (2) "Florida Cattle Ranching," Florida Memory, tinyurl.com/y62vl63x; (3) information provided by Dan Autrey III; (4) Jim Robison, "Sharing Tales of Early Settlers will Preserve St. Cloud's Past," *Orlando Sentinel*, April 21, 2002, tinyurl.com/qvbhnax (subscription required); and (5) Rowland Stiteler, "The Last of the Cowboys: Geech Partin and the Partin Clan," *Orlando Sentinel*, November 23, 1986, tinyurl.com/yywpg96o (subscription required).

Chapter 8 Katie

1. The term *doula* comes from the ancient Greek word meaning "female helper" or "maidservant." Throughout history, women have traditionally supported a woman through labor and birth. A modern doula is trained (and usually certified) to provide continuous physical, emotional, and informational support to a mother before, during, and shortly after childbirth to help her achieve the healthiest, most satisfying experience possible. Many scientific studies examining doula care demonstrate remarkably improved physical and psychological outcomes for both mother and baby (see www.DONA.org for more information).
2. Horatio Gates Spafford, "It Is Well with My Soul," 1873, public domain, Wikipedia, https://en.wikipedia.org/wiki/It_Is_Well_with_My_Soul.

Chapter 9 The Journey

1. Paul Brand and Philip Yancey, *Fearfully and Wonderfully Made: A Surgeon Looks at the Human and Spiritual Body* (Grand Rapids: Zondervan, 1984).

Chapter 10 Our Town

1. For this conversation, I refreshed my memory with the following: (1) "Osceola Wild Turkey," Sports Globe, tinyurl.com/y53kn864; (2) "Osceola Seminole Warrior Leader," Osceola County, tinyurl.com/y2vnn7ye; (3) "Seminole Chief Osceola, Billy Powell," Native Heritage Project, May 10, 2014, tinyurl.com/yy9vogwx; and (4) an email exchange with Anza and Michael Bast.

2. For this chapter, I refreshed my memory with the following: (1) "Makinson Hardware—Oldest in the State of Florida," Osceola County, tinyurl.com /yxo9c2h5; (2) Annie Tin, "Five-and-Dime's Demise Saddens Loyal Customers," *Orlando Sentinel*, June 16, 1990, tinyurl.com/uyr6k8q (subscription required); (3) "1890: The Red Brick Courthouse," Ninth Judicial Circuit Court of Florida, tinyurl.com/y5cduufs; (4) "Monument of States," Wikipedia, tinyurl.com/wwkh 7yy; (5) Roobini Aruleswaran, "Tupper and Wise—Inventive and Innovative," Innovation Excellence, tinyurl.com/yxq5psqn; (6) "From Tails to Tales: Stalking a Dream," Gatorland, tinyurl.com/ycofdwmd; (7) Lauren McFaul, "Reptiles Get Star Status at Gatorland," *Orlando Sentinel*, October 13, 1984, tinyurl.com/y33 qwdk4 (subscription required); and (8) "Osceola County History: A Step Back in Time," an insert supplement to the *Osceola News-Gazette*, January 20, 2020.

Chapter 11 Commencement

1. 1 Thessalonians 5:16–18.

Chapter 12 Forgiveness

1. Ephesians 4:32.

Chapter 13 Funeral

1. For this chapter, I refreshed my memory with the following: (1) Elaine Aradillas, "Jennings L. Overstreet, Osceola Ranching Pioneer, Dies at 70," *Orlando Sentinel*, October 8, 2005, tinyurl.com/y49eujra (subscription required); (2) Sandra Mathers, "'Boots' Autrey Left Her Mark on Osceola," *Orlando Sentinel*, May 23, 1997, tinyurl.com/y6hj8bzm (subscription required); (3) "History of Rodeo," 2013 PRCA Media Guide, 18, tinyurl.com/yx4dduaf; (4) Rowland Stiteler, "The Last of the Cowboys," *Orlando Sentinel*, November 23, 1986, tiny url.com/yywpg96o (subscription required); and (5) Rowland Stiteler, "The Last of the Cowboys," November 23, 1986, Sons of Confederate Veterans, tinyurl .com/y4ydw5ex.

Chapter 14 Hummingbird

1. Acts 17:11.
2. For this chapter, I refreshed my memory with the following: (1) Dan Autrey, "My Hummingbird," an unpublished account written by Dan Autrey and provided by Boots's daughter, Debby Cody, via scan and personal email, October 18, 2019; and (2) Tom Pinnock, "Architect Who Built Kissimmee," *Orlando Sentinel*, December 8, 1985, tinyurl.com/yyu596tl (subscription required).

Chapter 15 A New Home

1. For this chapter, I refreshed my memory with the following: (1) Louis M. Iatarola, "The Life and Influence of Hamilton Disston," Historical Society of

Tacony, June 8, 2009, tinyurl.com/y4txj25q; (2) "Silver Spurs Rodeo History," Silver Spurs Rodeo, tinyurl.com/y6nlsus9; (3) Katie Powalski, "Russell Thacker, 88, Took Public Service in Stride, Serving as Mayor," *Orlando Sentinel*, February 6, 2008, tinyurl.com/y5ev4kxr (subscription required); (4) Bob Kealing, *Tupperware, Unsealed: Brownie Wise, Earl Tupper, and the Home Party Pioneers* (Gainesville, FL, University of Florida Press, 2008); and (5) "Tupper Purchases Home on Lake," *Kissimmee Gazette* 59, no. 8 (November 14, 1952), 1 (front page provided by Anza Bast of the Osceola County Historical Society); "Which Home Is Finest in This Section," *Kissimmee Valley Gazette*, July 16, 1925, 2 (provided by Anza Bast of the Osceola County Historical Society).

2. 1 Timothy 5:8.

3. Matthew 6:24.

4. Philippians 2:3–4.

5. Psalm 127:3, 5.

Chapter 16 Brother Bill

1. Conway Twitty, "Don't Call Him a Cowboy," track 1 on *Don't Call Him a Cowboy*, 1985.

2. For this chapter, I've refreshed my memory with the following: (1) an interview with Bill Judge; and (2) "1991 Dairy Hall of Fame Inductee: Bryan William Judge, Jr., Judge Farms," a picture of an uncited article in Mr. Judge's home office in Kissimmee, FL.

Chapter 17 Practical Advice

1. 2 Timothy 2:2.

2. 1 Corinthians 6:19.

Chapter 19 Carpe Duh!

1. James C. Dobson, *Solid Answers: America's Foremost Family Counselor Responds to Tough Questions Facing Today's Families* (Wheaton: Tyndale, 1997).

Chapter 21 Iron Will

1. James Dobson, *The New Strong-Willed Child* (Wheaton: Tyndale, 2004), x.

2. Exodus 20:13 KJV.

Chapter 22 First Rodeo

1. For this chapter, I refreshed my memory with the following: (1) Lawrence J. Lebowitz, "Merchant Survives Holocaust, Thrives in the Western World," *Orlando Sentinel*, July 6, 1989, tinyurl.com/yf4x3hgu (subscription required); (2) "Clem McSpadden," ProRodeo Hall of Fame, tinyurl.com /sfw9ovb; (3) "Clem McSpadden," Wikipedia, tinyurl.com/rk349cb; (4) Frank Carroll, "Bullfighter [Scott Ramsey] Isn't Clowning Around," *Orlando*

Sentinel, February 13, 2000, tinyurl.com/yykffpv6 (subscription required); (5) Frank Carroll, "Kissimmee Bullfighter [Scott Ramsey] in World Finals," *Orlando Sentinel*, October 21, 2001, tinyurl.com/y5b5hz5k (subscription required); (6) "Silver Spurs Rodeo History," Silver Spurs Rodeo, tinyurl.com/y6nlsus9; and (7) Christina Williams, "The Saddle Rack Rides into Sunset," *Orlando Sentinel*, January 25, 1998, tinyurl.com/yjyhun5m (subscription required).

Chapter 23 The Greatest Show

1. Clem McSpadden, "The Cowboy's Prayer," CowboyWay, tinyurl.com/yhdeao2.

2. For this chapter, I refreshed my memory with the following: (1) "History of Rodeo," 2013 PRCA Media Guide, 18, ProRodeo, tinyurl.com/yx4dduaf; and (2) "Silver Spurs Rodeo History," Silver Spurs Rodeo, tinyurl.com/y6nlsus9.

Chapter 24 Professors

1. Mother Teresa, "20 Touching Pearls of Wisdom from Mother Teresa," Bright Side, tinyurl.com/y5ykxu8l.

Chapter 25 Friends

1. Romans 8:28.

Chapter 26 Dunkin'

1. John 16:7–9 NLT.

Chapter 27 Birthing

1. 2 Samuel 12:24 ESV.
2. 2 Samuel 12:22–23 ESV.
3. 2 Corinthians 1:3 RSV-CE.
4. 2 Corinthians 1:4 RSV-CE.
5. Spafford, "It Is Well with My Soul."

Chapter 28 A Curious Case

1. "Breastfeeding and the Use of Human Milk," *Pediatrics* 129, no. 3 (March 2012), tinyurl.com/y62z25qa.

Chapter 33 Patients Know

1. Richard Armour, "The Medical Muse," *Postgraduate Medicine* 23, no. 2 (1958): A154. Used with permission.
2. 3 John 1:2.

Chapter 34 Less Terrible

1. 1 Corinthians 13:4–8.
2. 1 John 1:9.
3. Ephesians 5:18.
4. Ephesians 5:19–20.
5. Galatians 5:22–23 NLT.
6. The first phrase of each of the eight couplets comes from: Donald Grey Barnhouse, "Donald Grey Barnhouse quotes," Good Reads, tinyurl.com/t2u uglu. Also quoted in James S. Hewett, ed., *Illustrations Unlimited* (Wheaton: Tyndale, 1988), 321. The second phrase of each of the eight couplets comes from George Campbell Morgan, The Westminster Pulpit, vol. 1: *The Preaching of G. Campbell Morgan* (Eugene, OR: Wipf & Stock, 2012), 166–79, tinyurl.com /vlu42lh, previously published by Fleming H. Revell in 1954.
7. Brother Lawrence (Nicholas Herman of Lorraine), *The Practice of the Presence of God* (London: H. R. Allenson, Ltd., 1906), 22.
8. 1 Corinthians 13:13.

Chapter 35 The Best Medicine

1. NKJV.
2. "Plaque: Lord Byron—Westminster plaque," London Remembers, tinyurl .com/rldae9g.

Chapter 36 A Rich Man

1. This chapter is adapted from Walt Larimore, MD, "The Wealthiest Man in Kissimmee," Focus on the Family's *Physician* magazine (July/August 1995): 18–19.
2. 2 Corinthians 12:7.

Chapter 37 A New Man

1. Romans 6:23.
2. Romans 3:23.
3. John 10:10.
4. Romans 6:23 ESV.
5. John 17:3.
6. John 14:6.
7. John 6:44.
8. 1 John 1:9 ESV.
9. John 1:12.
10. Philippians 1:18–21 RSV-CE.
11. John 14:2 NKJV.
12. Jeremiah 1:5.
13. Revelation 21:4 NLT.
14. 2 Peter 3:9; Revelation 1:1; 22:20.

Chapter 38 Extraordinary Birthdays

1. 2 Samuel 12:7.
2. 2 Samuel 12:13.
3. 2 Samuel 12:1.
4. 1 John 2:15–17.
5. Proverbs 3:5–6 NLT.

Chapter 39 Eternal Significance

1. C. S. Lewis, *Mere Christianity* (San Francisco: HarperSanFrancisco, 2001), 136–37.
2. Psalm 16:11 ESV.
3. Matthew 25:14–30; Mark 13:34; Luke 19:12–27.
4. Luke 19:17 ESV.
5. Oswald Chambers, "September 2: A Life of Pure and Holy Sacrifice," *My Utmost for His Highest* (New York: Dodd, Mead & Co, 1963); Utmost, tinyurl.com/yxgezusb.

Chapter 40 Graduate with Honors

1. John 10:10.
2. Galatians 5:22–23 NLT.
3. Luke 9:23 MSG.
4. McSpadden, "The Cowboy's Prayer."
5. "The Declaration of Independence," US History, tinyurl.com/sb7c56h.
6. Robert Anson Heinlein, *Time Enough for Love: The Lives of Lazarus Long* (New York: E. F. Putnam and Sons, 1973), 265–66.
7. Psalm 92:12–14.
8. Adapted from Philippians 3:13 NLT.

Acknowledgments

1. Jay Siwek, MD, "Editorial: 'Family Physician's Notebook': A New Feature," *American Family Physician* 42, no. 1 (July 1990).
2. Janis Wright, "Pearls in the Muck," *American Family Physician* 59, no. 1 (January 1, 1999): 9, tinyurl.com/qrtkvrm.
3. Wright, "Pearls in the Muck," 9.
4. Lois Johnson Rew, *Editing for Writers* (New York: Pearson, 1998).

Coming in 2021

*The Continuing Tales of
Dr. Walt, His Family, and
His and Dr. John's
Small-Town Practice*

I WAS IN SCRUBS racing to the hospital in my old pickup truck in the middle of a cool, moonless night. The ER had paged me to see a patient complaining of severe chest pain. As I skidded around the corner onto Oak Street, I saw scores of flashing lights a few blocks ahead. I drove up to see if I might help and parked behind a group of fire trucks, police cars, and an ambulance.

On the other side of a deeply gouged residential front lawn, a police cruiser had crashed into an oak tree. Its front end was wrapped around the massive trunk, and the dashboard was thrust back, pinning the motionless driver in a cab filled with smoke. A burning stench permeated the air while steam hissed from the engine compartment. There was no visible fire. The remnants of fire-suppressing foam covered the front of the car and the surrounding lawn. The air was contaminated with the scent of burned rubber and oil.

I walked over and recognized Chief Frank Ross, standing not far from the vehicle. "What in the world happened?" I asked.

"One of my men was on patrol. Must have fallen asleep. He's not in good shape, and he's pinned in."

"Chief, can I help? In North Carolina, I had medical rescue and extraction training."

"Just might need you."

Firefighters with hoses were at the front and back of the car, while two firemen were positioning their Jaws of Life—a hydraulic tool used by emergency rescue personnel to assist vehicle extrication of a crash victim.

Frank commented, "The EMTs stopped the bleeding from a bad head wound and splinted what they think is a broken wrist. But the wreckage has crushed and pinned his leg. They'll use the

Jaws to remove both front doors, which you can see are crumbled and inoperable. Dr. Gonzales, who serves as the police department surgeon, is on his way. May have to amputate his lower leg to get him out."

The metal squealed and creaked as the Jaws pried open the driver's door. The men backed away, indicating to the chief it was safe. "You mind checking him out?" Frank asked.

"Not at all. Who is it?"

"Gib. Gib Michaels."

I crouched next to Gib and found him unresponsive. His still-buckled seat belt held him upright. He had a cervical collar on his neck and a bloodied bandage around his forehead and scalp. Dried blood stained the front of his face, neck, and uniform, while a pool had soaked his lap.

"Vitals are stable, Doc," an EMT said from behind me. "Bad forehead laceration—to the bone—but the bleeding stopped with direct pressure."

"Got a bright light?"

He handed me a small flashlight, and I confirmed his observation. "Pupils equal and respond briskly. But he's unresponsive. Severe concussion at the very least—maybe worse." Gib had a wrist splint on his left arm.

"Got a pulse?" the EMT asked.

"Checking now."

I unhooked the Velcro and took off the brace. His wrist cocked up at a hideous angle. It was a fracture I had seen many times in folks who fall and land on the heel of their palm with the wrist extended. It's called a FOOSH—a Fall On Outstretched Hand type of fracture. Here, it was most likely from hitting the steering wheel or dashboard during the crash. His hand was ice cold. I tried to find a radial or ulnar pulse, but to my horror could feel no pulse on either side. I knew I had no choice but to reduce the fracture as much as possible. Otherwise, Gib could lose his hand. I had done these many times in my short career but never in this scenario.

The Jaws of Life fired up, and the passenger side door was pried away. Pete Gonzalez crawled in. I explained my assessment and plan. He nodded. "Do it."

I grasped Gib's left wrist with my right hand and then grabbed his left hand with my left hand as if we were shaking hands. I then pulled his hand away from his body while further extending his wrist, to unlock the compressed ends of the large forearm bone—the radius. Then, while pulling as hard as I could, I flexed the wrist and deviated it outward. The bones crunched against each other as Gib yelled in pain, but the reduction worked. The deformity was gone. "His pulse is back!" I exclaimed to Pete. "His hand is warming up."

"Good job!" Pete said as Gib moaned. "That may have been what we needed to wake up our officer."

"Gib!" I yelled, gently slapping his cheek. "Officer Michaels!"

"Quit yelling at me!" he responded. "I can hear you. What happened?"

He had no recollection of the entire evening. It's what we call *retrograde amnesia*, a sure sign of a traumatic brain injury in which one loses short-term but not long-term memory—as was evident with his next statement. "Are you the doctor with the ugly truck?"

"Guilty," I said, as Pete and I both chuckled. "In fact, it's not fifty feet from us now."

"Better watch out, Doc," he said. "Chief Ross is likely to have that fool thing towed off!" He smiled. It was a great smile to see.

"Let's see if we can get him out," Pete said. "I've done more than my share of these types of extractions during my MASH days in Vietnam and more than once on highways around here." He shined a flashlight into the mangled wreckage at Gib's feet. "Looks like his right lower leg is crushed and lacerated by debris."

Pete turned and requested leather gloves for each of us. With them on, we contorted ourselves into position to explore the twisted metal, rubber, and interior upholstery that had trapped his leg and, to our surprise, were able to work our hands up and around his lower leg and foot. We somehow pulled back enough debris to free Gib's leg, although it began bleeding.

"Hold direct pressure!" Pete ordered. As I did, I could feel the splintered ends of Gib's tibia and fibula sticking out through the skin. Pete turned and yelled, "Tourniquet! Stat!" One of the EMTs handed him one, and he placed it just below Gib's knee and cinched it up. "Let go of the pressure, Walt." I did, and the bleeding had stopped.

"Walt, you secure the leg. I will let the boys get in here and cut him out of his seat belt. Then we'll extract him from this side, and you follow. But keep pulling to distract the bones. That will help pull them back and set them."

"This is gonna hurt, isn't it?" Gib asked.

"Like the dickens!" Pete answered.

"Can I get a pain shot before you do any more?"

"I'd love to Officer," Pete answered. "But we have to have you awake. We may need your help."

Just then, someone outside yelled, "Fire!"

I looked up to see flames in the engine compartment. I barely had time to clench my eyes shut and duck my head as a fireball rocked the car.

Walt Larimore, MD, has been a family physician for nearly forty years. He is the bestselling author of the Bryson City books, as well as nearly three dozen other books and over a thousand articles in many magazines and journals. He has been called "one of America's best-known family physicians," was the recipient of a lifetime achievement award from Marquis Who's Who in America in 2019, and has been listed in *Distinguished Physicians of America*, *The Best Doctors in America*, and the *Guide to America's Top Family Doctors*. He writes a bimonthly health column, "Ask Dr. Walt," for *Today's Christian Living* magazine, and he formerly hosted the *Ask the Family Doctor* show on Fox's Health Network and the *Focus on Your Family's Health* radio program while serving as vice president at Focus on the Family. Dr. Larimore and his wife of forty-seven years have two adult children and two adorable granddaughters and reside in Colorado Springs, Colorado.

CONNECT WITH DR. WALT

To learn more about Walt Larimore, MD, and read his blogs, visit

DRWALT.COM